The Actor-Managers

The
Actor-Managers

Frances Donaldson

WEIDENFELD AND NICOLSON

5 Winsley Street London W1

SBN 297 00154 X

Printed in Great Britain by
Willmer Brothers Limited, Birkenhead

Contents

Illustrations

Except where otherwise stated, all photographs were provided by the Raymond Mander and Joe Mitchenson Theatre Collection.

Acknowledgements

I would like to acknowledge the sources listed below for granting me permission to reproduce quotations from the books mentioned after their names.

Ernest Benn Ltd (*A Player Under Three Reigns*, Sir Johnston Forbes-Robertson); The Bodley Head (*Ellen Terry and Bernard Shaw: A Correspondence*, ed. Christopher St John); Curtis Brown Ltd (*Gerald, A Portrait*, Daphne du Maurier and *Henry Beerbohm Tree, Some Memories of Him and of His Art*, ed. Max Beerbohm); Granada Publishing (*Around Theatres*, Max Beerbohm); Laurence Irving (*Henry Irving: The Actor and His World*); Macmillan & Co (*The Bancrofts On and Off the Stage, By Themselves*); John Murray Ltd (*The Bancrofts*, Squire and Marie Bancroft); Gilbert Samuel & Co (*Ellen Terry's Memoirs* and *Ellen Terry*, Roger Manvell); Society of Authors (*Ellen Terry and Bernard Shaw, A Correspondence*, ed. Christopher St John and *Our Theatres in the Nineties*, Bernard Shaw); A. P. Watt & Son (*Beerbohm Tree: His Life and Laughter*, Hesketh Pearson).

Throughout I have made great use of *Our Theatres in the Nineties* by George Bernard Shaw, and *Around Theatres*, by Max Beerbohm. There is a short bibliography of the other books from which I have quoted or which I have found particularly valuable at the end of the book.

The BBC kindly granted me permission to quote a passage from the transcript of the television programme *Omnibus*, and the Raymond Mander and Joe Mitchenson Theatre Collection gave me valuable advice and help with the illustrations.

Frances Donaldson

Introduction

The great years of the actor-managers were from 1865 to 1914, although the climate remained sufficiently favourable to them into the 1920s. Actors have a natural desire to form their own companies and impose their own style on productions, and the actor as manager was not unknown before this time and will probably always occasionally appear. Earlier, however, the area of opportunity was exceedingly small, and latterly the management of a theatre has become a financial undertaking of such magnitude that it is not easily performed as an occupation secondary to that of a particularly demanding art. But, in any case, the actor in management today is merely a man who combines, usually for a comparatively short period, two normally separate functions. In the late nineteenth and early twentieth centuries he was a power in the land and a social phenomenon of unusual interest and charm.

The pride and the place of the actor-manager were comparable then to those of men born to a great hereditary position; the companies of actors were like small courts to the heads of the profession and the public their willing slaves. When Irving died the streets were lined with people who silently watched his last journey to Westminister Abbey. Nowadays bravura is sadly out of fashion, but men were not believed equal then, stars shone without impropriety on their fellows, and acting was expected of the actor, both on and off the stage.

Because the position of the actor-manager was so exalted, it was heavily guarded. As a result, young actors with unusual gifts had often little choice between chancing their own arm in management – with all the attendant risks but with all the

additions to personality that success in the role would bring –
or restricting their performances to a few lines spoken in the
shade of some existing luminary. The play was not the thing.

That is the key to an understanding of the period. By the
middle of the nineteenth century no literary figure of distinction was writing for the theatre. Such new plays as were put on
were mostly melodrama, adaptations from the French, or
farce, knocked together by literary hacks. Two things
followed. Plays were seldom put on for a 'run'; instead the
extensive bills were frequently changed, and, secondly, play-
goers went to the theatre, not so much to see a new play, as
to see a new actor in an old play. Actors were expected to
make their mark in the roles of their predecessors, and play-
goers went regularly to the theatre to see them perform not
merely such roles as Hamlet or Sir Peter Teazle but others such
as Claude Melnotte in *The Lady of Lyons*, *Robert Macaire*, or
Kean's old role of Sir Giles Overreach in *A New Way to Pay
Old Debts*.

Many of these plays seem today meretricious and silly, and
it is difficult to understand how audiences could sit through
them again and again unless one realises that the audiences of
the mid-nineteenth century were no more disturbed by the conventions of the old-fashioned drama than are the audiences of
today by the conventions of opera and ballet. The comparison
is valid in more ways than one. The opera-goer of today does
not refuse to go to *La Traviata* because he has seen it before or
to *Figaro* because the characters recognise each other or fail to
recognise each other when dressed to resemble some other
character to suit the convenience of the plot. On the contrary
he is more willing to hear a new singer in an old role than to
hear a new work; and often he takes pleasure in a new production just to see how these absurd old situations have been
treated. This comparison falls to the ground when we stop to
remember that the really vital element in opera is the genius of
the composer, but it nevertheless remains true that we can
better understand the Victorian theatre if we bear it in mind.

In a situation of this sort the actor is everything, and he is
conscious that it is he who draws the crowds into the theatre
and is concerned to find roles that will allow him to show him-

self off at his best. He chooses a play because it is a vehicle
for the art of acting not because it is art itself.

It has sometimes been said that the lives of actors are not of
interest after they are dead because their art dies with them.
If this were true it would be a rather curious exception to the
general rule that the lives of human beings, particularly exceptional human beings or those that lived in an earlier age, are
always of interest to their fellows. But the question of quality
arises. If we are to involve ourselves, even for a short while
and purely for entertainment, with the life of some man long
dead, we want to know that he was worth our attention. If he
was an actor and his life is presented to us because he was an
actor we want to be sure he was a good one. It is precisely
here that, before the invention of the moving pictures,
assurance was hard to find. Desmond MacCarthy wrote 'The
triumphs of dead actors live for us only in pictures, in half-
obliterated tradition, and in the pages of the few dramatic
critics who happen to be still readable on account of their style.'

Of these three, 'half-obliterated tradition' plays the greatest
part. One actor passes his method on to another actor and in
this way the body of technique is built up. But 'half-obliterated
tradition' is no more available to the historian or biographer
than the art of the actor himself. For a lively impression we
have to depend on 'pictures . . . and . . . the pages of the few
dramatic critics who happen to be still readable on account of
their style.'

Max Beerbohm complained that the biographies of actors are
too often undertaken by 'some hack-journalist who knew the
deceased slightly, or . . . some pious understrapper who knew
him too well, in too special relationship to have the faintest
notion of what roundly he was like', and although in recent
years several excellent biographies of Victorian actors have
appeared, to recapture the quality of their acting we still
depend on contemporary accounts. Fortunately in the heyday
of the actor-managers several writers of great distinction were
interesting themselves in the theatre.

Since the earlier history of the theatre had great influence on
that of the nineteenth century some knowledge of it is necessary to an understanding of the latter. The Puritans attempted

to suppress the drama altogether and when, at the Restoration, Charles II renewed the right to put on plays he did so by granting a licence to two of his courtiers to form companies of actors and present plays. These licences were handed on from one man to another and in the course of time were sold, but they came to be vested in the two theatres at Covent Garden and Drury Lane, and only in these two great patent houses could drama be legally performed.

This was a situation which made it practically certain that the bad would drive out the good. The drama could thrive only when one or both the houses were well and successfully managed, while the standards of each could be dragged by the standards of the other towards the popular taste. Success at one house often meant a policy of circuses at the other, and this in its turn forced circuses on the first. The policy of the patent houses was dictated by the people of London.

Inevitably the licensing laws were not kept, and it was largely in the breaking of them that, in the eighteenth and early nineteenth centuries, traditions developed to which the actor-managers succeeded. New methods to evade the law were continually invented. Plays were performed between two halves of a concert and, because musical plays could be performed without licence, a play could be put on at any theatre providing there were five songs to each act. Shakespeare was often performed with musical interpolations and sometimes the law was acknowledged by no more than a chord struck at regular intervals. At the same time the patents, originally given to revive the drama, became no more than a commercial monopoly of the right to put it on, and although the managers of the two patent houses bitterly opposed any attempt to alter the law they could no more afford to disregard the public demand for music and spectacle than could the managers of the little theatres which by now were springing up all over London.

In the provinces the law was not so severely enforced and patent houses were established at many of the main towns during the eighteenth century. A system developed called the 'Circuit' system whereby companies of actors adopted certain towns in their district, eventually building small theatres in them. At these theatres the resident company, called the 'stock' company, was ready to play the parts in a whole repertory of plays, while the leading parts were played by visitors, in summer by great stars from London. In the stock companies each actor undertook a particular type of role. In addition to a Leading Man, a Juvenile Lead and a Leading Lady, every company included such types as a Low Comedian, a Heavy Father, a Chamber Maid, later to be known as a Soubrette, Walking Ladies and Gentlemen, later to be known as Supernumeraries or Supers, all terms that have passed into the English language.

These stock companies were the only schools for young actors and here they learned, not how to interpret the ideas of the playwright in terms of human character, but how to present the 'stock' figure. Bernard Shaw said that the playgoers in their towns grew so desperately tired of the actors in a stock company, and so unable to imagine them to be anything but their too-familiar selves that 'they performed in an atmosphere of hatred and derision which few of their members had talent or charm enough to conciliate'.

Both in London and in the country actors were excessively badly paid and often starving. They received part of their salary through the 'benefit' system, by which the profits of the theatre were given on a particular night to one, sometimes two, of the actors. These actors were allowed to choose the play in which they would appear and were supported by their fellows. Obviously the 'benefit' of a leading and popular actor would be very much more profitable than that of a struggling small-part player, and it was a vicious system which caused much humiliation and hardship.

At last in 1843 an Act for Regulating the Theatres made an end of the patent system and for the first time, if certain conditions were observed, plays might legally be performed all over England. But by now the theatre had fallen very low and the twenty years that followed have been described as 'the winter solstice' of the British drama. In terms of a serious art, there were no playwrights, no school of acting, above all no audience. The middle and upper classes no longer went to the theatre except to hear Italian opera, and the managers of the theatres had learned that to entice people in they had continually to change the bill and must compete with acrobats, performing animals, hippodramas, panoramas, spectacle of every kind. The theatregoers of the time insisted on bills of inordinate length and there were curtain-raisers and epilogues, burlesques and burlettas, while even Shakespeare's plays were put on with at least two other entertainments in the bill. Conditions in the theatre were such that contemporary writers complained it was merely an ancillary to the brothels.

Thus was the scene set when the Bancrofts appeared upon it.

Sir Squire and Lady Bancroft
1841-1926 & 1839-1921

In the years immediately following the First World War a married couple of great distinction and extreme age were sometimes to be seen in the foyers of London theatres or the dining room of one of the leading hotels in Folkestone – he with a truly leonine shock of completely white hair, a white moustache and an eyeglass, she a small pouter pigeon surviving from the reign of Queen Victoria. To an onlooker it might have been apparent that this couple were treated with a deference exceeding that to which their age alone entitled them, but if so he would not have been able to account for this by associating them with some public role. This was not because there had never been a public role but because it had been performed so long ago that only the initiated would now know Sir Squire and Lady Bancroft, and remember that in their day they had been responsible for a small revolution in the English theatre.

We have learned a great deal of what is known about this couple from themselves, because in their old age they told their own story at such length and with so much detail that little was left for anyone else to say. There is plenty of corroboration for the claims they make, however, and, combined with a rather absurd pomposity, there is an essential modesty, a straightforward honesty in the manner of the telling.

Place aux dames. Lady Bancroft begins her part of the joint biography with these words and it is a fact that the first of our actor-managers was a woman. However, this is only one of several ways in which this management was untypical of the heroic age of the Victorian theatre. The Bancrofts are taken first because they were first in time and also because their innovations provided the groundwork for a whole edifice, but they do not completely illustrate either the characteristic actor-manager of the time or the description of him in the introductory chapter to this book.

Marie Wilton was born in 1839, not to one of the old theatre families but to parents who had, nevertheless, both been disastrously connected with the stage. Her father, a gentleman from Gloucestershire, had been intended for the church but in early life he was stage-struck, and in spite of the many obstacles put in his way, became in the end an actor and, in the words of his daughter, 'an exile from home, family, friends and general respectability'. On the stage he found neither fame nor fortune to compensate for the loss of these things, but he met and married a Miss Faulkner, the daughter of a scholar and a gentleman who had lost all his money by investing it in the York Theatre Circuit. Miss Faulkner eloped with Mr Wilton and they lived in poverty and anxiety for the rest of their lives.

Not so their daughter. Lady Bancroft tells in her autobiography of the time when as a baby she cried and moaned inconsolably all night. In the morning it was discovered that her body was completely covered with finger-and-thumb marks as though it had been pinched. That day, as her mother, unable to quiet her cries, despairingly rocked her in her arms, an old peasant woman entered their garden to sell her wares. When, in response to questions, the mother showed her baby's body with the pinch-marks on it, the old woman declared the child had been bewitched. She predicted that at sunset the marks would disappear and the child would grow to be the luckiest in the world. 'She'll tell of things before they come to pass and bring good to them she wishes to and woe to them as wrongs her.'

In her last years Lady Bancroft used still to tell this story, and it was clear that, followed by good fortune all her life, she much more than half believed in the pinch-marks and the interpretation put upon them by the gypsy, just as she believed in the powers of the black cats which had so often crossed her path on her way to the theatre.

But if she had more than her share of good luck Marie Wilton had to work for it from the earliest age. One of the favourite turns in the long bills demanded by the public in those days was that of the child actor, and Marie Wilton was set to earn her living on the stage before she could even speak properly. Among the recitations with which the little girl was taught to edify her public were the trial scene from *The Merchant of Venice*, the balcony scene from *Romeo and Juliet*, and the sleep-walking scene from *Macbeth*.

Her family depended on her earnings and, like the children who worked in the factories, she was dragged from her bed to go to the theatre and returned to it, weary in temper and limb, long after most children were sound asleep. When not actually performing she was endlessly coached by her parents. She tells us that her father and mother stood one in each wing during her performances, her father prompting her with the line she should speak, her mother assuming the expression she should wear upon her face. Although her father had no talent for acting, her mother had great gifts as a teacher. Marie profited from the teaching, but she possessed the talent her father lacked and it is clear that she was a born comedienne.

As she grew older she abandoned her recitations and took part in the performance of plays. Once she played Fleance to Macready's Macbeth, and once she played Prince Arthur in *King John* while Charles Kemble sat watching in a box. Both these great actors sent for her at the close of the performance and both gave her a piece of advice. Macready, upon asking her what part she hoped to play when she had grown to be a great actress, received the reply: 'Lady Macbeth.'

'Do not,' he said to her, 'play Lady Macbeth too soon; begin slowly or you may end quickly!'

And when Charles Kemble sent for her he advised her:

'Climb not the ladder too quickly, or you may come suddenly to the ground again.'

Sir John Gielgud has said he believes it takes fifteen years to make an actor. Marie Wilton had no difficulty in following the advice of these great practitioners because, born with a talent for acting and a capacity for hard work, she had been fifteen years on the stage at an age when most young actresses have hardly started their careers. When she was still a child she and her mother left her father in Bristol and travelled to London so that she might take up an engagement at the Lyceum. From this time onwards she had one engagement after another on the London stage.

She seems only twice in her life to have been seriously thwarted. The first time was when, still a child, she was cast again and again in the role of Cupid until she feared she was going to spend the whole of her professional life appearing through trapdoors from unexpected and impossible places. The second time was when as a young woman she seemed to be doomed to play boys in burlesque for the rest of her life.

The burlesque is a dramatic form with a distinguished history. The first and most famous burlesque was *The Rehearsal* (1671) written by the Duke of Buckingham in parody of the pseudo-heroic plays in rhyming verse of which Dryden was the master. Buckingham parodied playwrights, actors and critics and he personally coached the actor who played the part of Bayes, the author, to mimic Dryden's rather eccentric speech and gestures. Dryden accepted the hit in silence at the time but later he returned it in full in *Absalom and Achitophel*. *The Rehearsal* became a theatrical sensation for the second time when the young David Garrick discarded the traditional imitation of Dryden and parodied instead the style of each of the leading actors of the day. Burlesque became a recognised dramatic form of which other famous examples are Gay's *The Beggar's Opera*, *Tom Thumb* by Henry Fielding and Sheridan's *The Critic*, but by the nineteenth century the satiric impulse had been lost and it had degenerated into light musical entertainment. Usually it was still related to the plot of some popular play, but male and female impersonators had become part of the comic tradition and by the time Marie Wilton grew up, burlesque was little more than a vehicle for the execrable puns so much relished by Victorian audiences. Many of the most popular burlesques of the day were by H. J. Byron, and a good idea of the spirit of the thing can be gained merely from the programme of *Lucia di Lammermoor; or the Laird, the Lady and the Lover*, which he wrote for the Prince of Wales's Theatre company:

HENRY ASHTON (an *ash-tonishingly* revengeful party, who in depth and bitterness acts up to his character as a Bass-o-profundo)
Mr. F. Dewar.

DR. RAYMOND (his guide, philosopher and friend, tutor to Lucy, physician to the family, accustomed to dog Henry and dog-Latin)
Mr. H. W. Montgomery.

EDGAR OF RAVENSWOOD (an interesting young operatic hero of the regular conventional type whom Henry attempts to make a butt of, but only succeeds in making a little pale)
Miss Marie Wilton.

NORMAN (Head Huntsman to Henry)
Mr. Harry Cox.

ARTHUR BUCKLAW (a great swell in his way, and also in Edgar's)
Miss Fanny Josephs.

LUCY of LAMMERMOOR (Henry's only sister, a simple dove-like creature given by her own admission to melancholy and by her brother to Bucklaw)
Mr. J. Clarke.

ALICE (her confidential maid, who, like all confidential people speaks her mind pretty freely to everybody)
Miss Hughes.

As a young girl Marie Wilton joined Miss Swanborough's company at the Strand Theatre, which was largely given over to burlesque. Here she played boys for so long that on being given the part of Pippo in *The Maid and the Magpie* she wrote to Miss Swanborough to ask if some change could be made in the cast. When Miss Swanborough saw her to discuss the matter she was accompanied by H. J. Byron, the author of the piece, then only a young man. He begged her to play Pippo, saying: 'I am only a beginner, you know, and this burlesque may make or mar me.'

Miss Wilton was unable to refuse a request so persuasively put, and the play proved a great success for both her and its author. At this time in her career we have a description of her written by Charles Dickens.

I really wish you would go to see *The Maid and the Magpie* burlesque. . . . There is the strangest thing in it that ever I have seen on the stage – the boy Pippo, by Miss Wilton. While it is astonishingly impudent (must be, or it couldn't be done at all), it is so stupendously like a boy, and unlike a woman, that it is perfectly free from offence. I never have seen such a thing. She does an imitation of the dancing of the Christy Minstrels – wonderfully clever – which, in the audacity of its thorough-going, is surprising.

A thing that you *cannot* imagine a woman doing at all; and yet
the manner, the appearance, the levity, impulse and spirits of it are
so exactly like a boy, that you cannot think of anything like her
sex in association with it. I never have seen such a curious thing,
and the girl's talent is unchallengeable. I call her the cleverest girl
I have ever seen on the stage in my time, and the most singularly
original.

Nevertheless Miss Wilton remained totally dissatisfied. She
had her heart set not merely on achieving the right to assert
her sex but on leaving burlesque behind her and playing
comedy. There were very few theatres at which comedy was
played, and when she applied to the managers of these she found
them enthusiastic to engage her – but to play boys in burlesque.

In despair she called one day on a married sister and her
husband, Mr and Mrs Francis Drake. When she explained to
them her position – not for the first time – Mr Drake said: 'I
see no chance for you but management. How would it be if
you had a theatre of your own?'

Marie Wilton replied confusedly that she could not take a
theatre without money, but her brother-in-law told her to
return the next day to discuss the matter again. At this second
interview he offered to lend her £1,000 if she could find a
theatre to let, and he said to her: 'Should you succeed you will
return the money, if you fail I will lose it.'

It was a large sum to risk on the young actress, who was at
this time twenty-six, but it must be remembered that Marie
Wilton had been providing for her sisters since she could first
walk on a stage, while her brother-in-law had presumably
already had some opportunity to observe the courage, judgment and originality she was later to show in management.

Her first action, once she had decided to take up her brother-
in-law's offer, was to ask H. J. Byron, now a very popular
writer, to go into partnership with her, giving her his exclusive
services as an author. Byron agreed, with the qualification that
as he was not in a position to put up any money he should be
indemnified against loss. Then a theatre had to be found. In
Tottenham Street off the Tottenham Court Road there was a
little theatre called the Queen's, at which in former days many
an illustrious actor and actress had appeared. But now it had
become a minor theatre in a bad part of the town, frequented

by a low kind of audience and nicknamed the Dusthole. It was not to let but the lessee Mr James was willing to come to some arrangement. Marie Wilton, against much advice since there was considerable doubt that the kind of audience she wished to attract could be induced to come to this theatre, proceeded to make an arrangement with him. She took possession of the theatre one month before she opened it, and during this time it was not merely cleaned and re-decorated but given new seats and new furniture. By the opening night the curtains and carpets and the new stalls were all pale blue, the latter covered with white anti-macassars.

Here are some details of the purchasing power of money at the time. After the complete transformation of the theatre £150 was left of the original £1,000. Marie Wilton had come to an arrangement by which she rented the theatre from Mr James and at the same time hired his services as acting-manager for £20 a week. She and Byron had agreed each to draw £10 a week as salary while she was to draw a further £10 a week as interest on her capital. This she paid to her brother-in-law. After these charges had been met the profits were to be shared equally between the two partners. When the theatre, re-named The Prince of Wales's Theatre, was first opened the price of a stall was 6s. Later it rose to 7s and still later to 10s. After two years Byron retired from the partnership, his place being filled by a young actor named Sidney Bancroft. Twenty years from the opening date Mr and Mrs Bancroft retired with a fortune of £180,000.

Marie Wilton and H. J. Byron were great favourites with the public but Miss Wilton was advised that while her aim in going into management was to finish with burlesque she could not afford to do this until she had established herself in the theatre. Her first programme therefore consisted of a comedietta called *The Winning Hazard*, followed by a burlesque of Mr Byron's, *La! Sonnambula! or the Supper, the Sleeper and the Merry Swiss Boy* (Miss Wilton played the Merry Swiss Boy), and a farce called *Vandyke Brown*.

The portents were, as usual with Miss Wilton, favourable. On the day that she opened, her mother, unable to stand the strain of remaining in London, went for a country drive to Willesden, accompanied by another of her daughters.

'What would I not give,' she said to her daughter, 'to know the end of this undertaking!' And, raising her eyes, she saw written on a signpost, 'Mary's Place, Fortune Gate'.

Sure enough the words were prophetic. Miss Wilton tells us that she never borrowed a further shilling in connection with this enterprise. 'I was successful in a modest way from the very first gradually but surely my lucky star led me on to fortune.'

All this time two young men were approaching the point when they would join Marie Wilton in a configuration happy for themselves and for the future of the British theatre.

In *Around Theatres* Max Beerbohm has an essay entitled 'The Invariable Badness of Amateur Acting' in which he asks why, since much may be said for the amateur in other arts, no one has ever beheld an amateur mime whose performance seemed comparable with even the worst professional performance. And he replies that there are no good amateur actors because acting is essentially a public art.

The fact that his work does not endure beyond the moment of its performance makes it essential for him [the actor] to be heard at large. . . . The man who has any real impulse for acting will not be satisfied with private or semi-private triumphs . . . will crave for a wider field. Consequently, he becomes a professional actor as soon as ever he can. And thus the amateur stage is always automatically deprived of such persons as might, if they tarried on it, become its ornaments.

Can this be true? one wonders. Does everyone with a talent for acting take to the professional stage? Is it so common for actors to discover this talent in amateur societies and then, depriving the amateur stage of all its ornaments, to give up all thought of another career?

At the time that Beerbohm was writing the stage had been given a measure of distinction and respectability, mainly by the actors and actresses whose lives are considered here, but this was new. For centuries the members of this profession had been regarded, if not as rogues and vagabonds, at least as low, licentious persons totally unfit to mix with the rest of the world. The fact that every great artist from Garrick to Irving was welcomed into London society should not mislead us as to the status of the ordinary member of the profession. No member of the middle or upper classes could contemplate with equanimity the prospect of a son or daughter joining the depraved company of the players, and any young man who wished to do so had to be willing to face, as Marie Wilton's father had, the prospect of being ostracised by his family. In addition actors were so badly paid that even men of talent had to be willing to struggle for years in poverty and wretchedness before they made their mark. 'Can you starve, cocky?' Edmund Kean is said to have asked a young man who came to ask his advice as to what he needed to do to become an actor, and not until the late nineteenth century did conditions begin to change for the better.

In consequence, it became a common thing for young men with talent for this outlawed art to honour their parents' wishes by sitting on an office stool all day, but to temper the ardour of their private longings by performing in the evening in one of the amateur companies which were a feature of Victorian society. When we read the lives of the great actors and actresses of that time we find that, while many of them came from old theatrical families and learned, like Marie Wilton, to act when they could barely walk, almost as many began as amateurs and only later succumbed to their craving for a wider field.

Sidney ('Squire') Bancroft did neither of these things. Born in 1841, two years later than the girl who was to become his wife and in the same year as King Edward VII and the magazine *Punch*, he was the son of a gentleman who died when he was a child, leaving his widow with very little money. As a result, he had to forego the education at public school and university for which he had been intended, although he seems to have been reasonably well educated, partly in England but also in France. As a child he was stage-struck and his toys were little theatres; as a youth, in spite of his mother's poverty, he seems to have been well enough endowed to go regularly to the play. He saw most of the leading actors of the day and, in addition, a child called Marie Wilton who made his mother and himself cry by her pathetic acting in *Belphegor* with Charles Dillon at the Lyceum.

When Bancroft was a young man, his mother died, and alone

in the world with no parent's heart to break or gladden, he determined to become an actor. He merely wrote to the lessees of all the leading provincial theatres and waited until one of them expressed a wish to see him. Then in 1861, with the smoothness which was to characterise his whole career, he was offered and accepted an engagement at twenty-one shillings a week from Mr Mercer Simpson at the Theatre Royal, Birmingham.

During his first season as an actor Squire Bancroft played thirty-six different parts, many of them in 'blood-and-thunder' plays. Towards the end of the season a visiting star, T. C. King, offered him an engagement in Cork for the Birmingham vacation and here he played forty fresh characters. Back in Birmingham again he played sixty-four parts in the next season, some of them with Phelps and some with G. V. Brooke. From here he went to Devonport and from there to Dublin, learning his profession as he travelled about the countryside, playing such parts as came his way. In Devonport he achieved a small amount of fame by an imitation of Edward Sothern, a famous actor of the day, as Lord Dundreary in *Our American Cousin*. Lord Dundreary was the first example of the caricature stage Englishman and one of the classics of its time. Squire Bancroft's youthful attendance at the theatre now paid him well because the manager of the theatre at Devonport, after watching him imitate Sothern for the benefit of his friends one night, prevailed upon him to repeat the performance publicly. Bancroft succeeded in filling a previously half-empty theatre. Then in Dublin he was praised by Charles Kean, who told him that were he still the lessee of a London theatre, 'it would be your own fault if you were not a member of my company'.

So he went on for several years learning his job in provincial companies in England and Ireland. During an engagement in Liverpool he met the celebrated burlesque company from the Strand theatre, which included Marie Wilton and a young actor called John Hare. Later Marie Wilton came to Liverpool again to play a short starring engagement before opening the Prince of Wales's with Mr Byron. She acted with Bancroft then for the first time and, as a spectator, watched her future husband play several parts. When she left Liverpool she and Byron offered Squire Bancroft an engagement in London. Writing of this time,

Squire Bancroft remarks that since he had refused several offers to appear in London, including one proposal to join Charles Fechter at the Lyceum, his decision to play burlesque in a speculative venture at a little, obscure theatre can be explained only by love at first sight. This may well be, but Bancroft was to find much besides love at this little theatre and it is not for his gifts as an actor that he is remembered today.

Miss Wilton had followed her successful opening bill with a comedy by H. J. Byron called *War to the Knife*, with which she again had a distinct success. In her second season her company was joined by John Hare[1] and her opening programme included a burlesque of *Lucia di Lammermoor*. Then Byron asked her to read a comedy by a friend of his called Tom Robertson. He told her quite frankly that the play had been turned down by numerous managements, partly because of a scene in a London pub called The Owl's Roost, in which the author had undisguisedly based his characters on journalists and critics of the day. London managers were nervous that this scene might give offence.

Miss Wilton, aged twenty-seven, with less than a full year in management, and very little money behind her, showed her courage and judgment by putting into rehearsal the play which so many established managements had turned down, coolly remarking that danger was better than dullness. On 11 November, 1865, *Society*, an original comedy by T. W. Robertson, opened at the Prince of Wales's Theatre, introducing a new theatrical style.

T. W. Robertson was born in 1829 and at the age of five became the fourth generation of his family to appear on the stage. His father was the manager of the Lincoln circuit and his mother an actress in that company. This couple had a very large family and it was said of them that they always had a juvenile stock company ready for any emergency. Their youngest child, Madge, who as Mrs Kendal was later to be famous on the London stage, made her first appearance in a play called *The Stranger* when she was four years old.

[1] Hare, Sir John, 1844–1921. Actor-manager. In management at the Court Theatre and afterwards in partnership with Mr and Mrs Kendal at the St James's. Knighted in 1907.

In his starveling youth Tom Robertson's life differed from
that of dozens of other children born to theatre families only
because he was immensely studious. He went to school as long
as his family could afford to send him there, acting only in the
holidays. But by the time he was fifteen business on the Lincoln
circuit had become so bad that he returned home to write plays
(he dramatised Christmas stories, among them those of Charles
Dickens), for a cast composed of his brothers and sisters, paint
scenery, manage, prompt and act in his father's company. As a
young man he went to Utrecht in the position of English-
speaking usher to a school, but this did no more for him than
to suggest later the character of Krux in *School*. He returned
to the stage, this time in London, and for many years he divided
his time between acting and writing, making from neither of
these occupations enough money to live in anything approaching comfort. As an actor he played everything from Shakespeare to farce, and as a writer he adapted plays in quantity
from the French, selling these to Thomas Lacy, a theatrical
publisher, the predecessor of Samuel French.

Not until he was thirty-six did he have any success with a
new play and then it was only a version from the French,
the theme of the play being one that had been used again and
again and described by Théophile Gautier as 'the everlasting
story of Garrick, Talma or Kean curing some foolish girl of a
passion for them as actors by exhibiting themselves in private
life under the most repulsive conditions'. In Robertson's version
it is Garrick who, meeting from the stage the gaze of a young
girl leaning out of a box at Drury Lane, is convinced that the
love he instantaneously feels is reciprocated. Later he is asked
by her father to use the art that has won her to disgust her so
much as to kill her unsuitable passion. In the next act Garrick
goes to dinner to meet the young lady and there plays the
drunken scene which made the part so attractive to generations
of leading actors. In Robertson's version the young lady, broken-
hearted in this act, discovers in the next that although the
drunkenness of the actor was an expression of the nobility of
his character, the young man she has now dutifully consented
to marry is really a drunkard. She then takes refuge with
Garrick. The play ends with the future of the romantic couple
in some doubt, left to the imagination of the audience. In a

preface to a novel on the same theme Robertson asserts that, although the incidents that occur in the book are not in accordance with biographical fact, they are not certainly untrue. They might have happened. That may be, but if to the taste of today it seems that the play might have been more effective if the leading character had been based on an imaginary rather than an actual figure, it is a fact that this story brought success to numberless writers, not least of them T. W. Robertson. David Garrick was played by Edward Sothern at the Haymarket Theatre and he continued to play the part to crowded audiences in London and the provinces for the rest of his acting career. Afterwards the role was taken over by Charles Wyndham, who played it not merely in England but also in Berlin, Moscow and St Petersburg.

Elated by the success of this play, Robertson immediately wrote for Sothern the part of Sydney Daryl in *Society*. But Buckstone, the manager of the Haymarket, declared that the piece was rubbish and refused to put it on. *Society* was then offered to most of the managements of London and finally, as we have seen, to Marie Wilton.

It was an immediate and great success. The pressure to get seats became so great that an extra row of stalls had to be added, and shortly after its opening the Prince of Wales paid the first of many visits to the theatre that had been named after him. *Society* was followed by another success, an original play by H. J. Byron called *A Hundred Thousand Pounds*, and this was followed by Robertson's second comedy for Miss Wilton's management, *Ours*.

In the year 1867 Byron, who had become involved in the management of the theatres in Liverpool, resigned from his partnership with Miss Wilton and in the same year she married Squire Bancroft.

The Bancrofts produced altogether six plays written by T. W. Robertson: *Society*, which ran originally for 150 nights, at that time an extraordinary run; *Ours*, which also ran for 150 nights; *Caste*, which ran 156 nights and was withdrawn while still playing to big houses because the Bancrofts were by now concerned to build up a repertory of plays that could be produced again and again *Play*, 106 nights; *School*, which was withdrawn after 380 performances still playing to full houses, and *M.P.*, which ran for about 160 nights and was succeeded by a revival of *Ours*. Throughout the course of the Bancrofts' management, both at the Prince of Wales's and later at the Haymarket, the Robertson comedies were revived again and again.

Robertson was in no sense of the word a great playwright. Henry James described his plays as 'infantile' and today the word seems not entirely inappropriate. It is, however, the fate of all but great plays to become increasingly childish as they grow older, and in this respect Robertson's plays do not seem more aged than many of fifteen, twenty or thirty years ago. It is significant that St Aldegonde, one of the most sophisticated young men in the whole of fiction, went 'in the most immoral manner' to see *School*, of which he had read in *Galignani*, on the first evening of his return from his travels, although Lothair was so displeased with this unfeeling conduct that he declined to accompany him.[2]

Robertson wrote small, neat plays, just as the Bancrofts were small, neat artists. The very attributes that make them unimportant today made them most striking in their time. In an age used to declamation, melodrama, spectacle, large theatres and romantic acting, Robertson wrote light comedies and the Bancrofts cast them with actors and actresses capable of giving comedy performances. Squire Bancroft quotes Garrick as saying to a young actor: 'You may humbug the town as a tragedian, but comedy is a serious thing, my boy, so don't try that just yet.'

As a result of his appearance in Robertson's plays Squire Bancroft became associated with a certain type of part – that of the well-dressed, drawling man about town – but there is every indication that he was a very good actor with a far wider range than his success in management gave him the chance to display. After his retirement from management he appeared at the Lyceum with Sir Henry Irving in a play called *The Dead Heart*.

'What a big name you might have made for yourself,' the great man remarked to him one night as they walked off stage, 'had you never come across those Robertson plays! What a

[2] The Earl of Beaconsfield (Benjamin Disraeli), *Lothair*, Hughenden Edition, p. 432.

pity, for your own sake; for no actor can be remembered long who does not appear in the classical drama.'

But Irving was wrong. Without Robertson Bancroft might have been one more great actor of classical drama; with him he is remembered not merely for his part in a revolution in theatrical productions but also for a revolution in theatrical customs.

The thing that most excites one's admiration for the Bancrofts is that in almost everything they did they ran counter to the spirit of the time. At a time when actor-managers chose plays for their value as a vehicle for their own talents and cast only minor actors in support of the main role, the Bancrofts chose and commissioned plays with a wide range of parts and cast them with the best actors they could find, often playing minor roles themselves. At a time when declamation was the order of the day, they introduced light comedy. At a time when actors and actresses were underpaid and harshly treated, they were known for their wise and benevolent management and for the introduction of a number of long-overdue reforms.

In speaking of the rehearsals of *Society* Marie Wilton says: 'My views of acting so entirely agreed with Mr Robertson's that we encountered no difficulties whatever, and everything went smoothly and merrily.' This is a remarkable fact, for Robertson's views on acting were very strong and completely original, while his views on production as carried out by the Bancrofts resulted in the introduction of modern scenic effects. Twenty years earlier Madame Vestris had used scenic cloths, carpets and elaborate furnishings, but it was left to the Bancrofts to employ these so successfully that they became an accepted part of theatrical productions. They put real rugs on the floor, real furniture on the sets, the rooms in which their performances took place had real ceilings and, which caused at the time the greatest sensation of all, real knobs on the door-handles. Their style became known as the 'cup-and-saucer' comedy because of the realistic effects in the kitchen scene in *Caste*. Before this time it was customary in a conversation scene merely to bring down two or three chairs to the middle of the stage for the actors to sit on while talking and afterwards to take them away. The Bancrofts earned theatrical fame for all these innovations but Tom Robertson had an equal responsibility.

W. S. Gilbert said that he 'invented' stage management and acknowledged that he had learned a great deal from him. George Rowell says in *The Victorian Theatre* that the appearance of the artistic director who was neither actor nor prompter marked a definite stage in the evolution of the modern producer or director, and that the dramatist-director was an influential factor in the late Victorian theatre, the succession passing from Robertson to Gilbert, to Pinero and ultimately to Shaw. And he points out that, although Robertson's own ideas were largely superficial, he did suggest how more forceful ideas could be given dramatic form.

Robertson more or less successfully killed the 'stock' character. Here are two of his stage directions:

The author requests this part may be played with a slight French accent. He is not to pronounce the words absurdly or duck his head towards his stomach like the conventional stage Frenchman.

And:

The actor playing Dunscombe is requested not to make too much of this situation. All that is required is a momentary memory of childhood – succeeded by the external phlegm of the man of the world. No tragedy, no tears, no pocket-handkerchief.

As actors, both Bancroft and John Hare paid tributes to Robertson, Hare saying that he had a gift peculiar to himself of 'conveying by some rapid and almost electrical suggestion to the actor an insight into the character assigned to him'.

Hare carried the Robertson style to the Court Theatre where he worked with Ellen Terry, and to the St James's where he was in partnership with the Kendals. Later actors such as Wyndham and Alexander developed Robertson's ideas, and so they passed into the tradition of acting. Writing to Squire Bancroft on the death of Lady Bancroft, Sir Arthur Pinero said:

The work of a writer for the stage should be judged in relation to the period which produced it, and, so judged, Robertson was a man of vision and courage. There is no dramatist now writing, 'advanced' or otherwise, who is not in a measure indebted to Robertson.

Without the Bancrofts Robertson might have made no mark of

any sort. His plays for other theatres showed none of the originality of the series of plays he wrote for them and are rather feeble in the sensational manner of the time. The Bancrofts were also responsible for many innovations in theatrical management. The little Prince of Wales's Theatre, with its carpeted auditorium and blue and white stalls, provided something new in London – an evening's entertainment suitable for the families of the middle and upper classes. Thus they laid the foundations for the change in status of the theatre which was to take place over the next twenty years.

At first they conformed to custom by including two or more items in their bills but, as they became certain of their audience and this came to consist more of the classes who dined late and preferred a shorter evening in the theatre, they gradually reduced the bill to the presentation of a single piece.

As early as 1867, they sent one of the first touring companies to travel the provinces in *Caste*. The railways now made it possible to transport scenery and properties, and gradually touring companies replaced the old resident 'stock' companies.

Another innovation for which they were partly responsible was the matinée. The Bancrofts first gave a morning performance of *School* but this was not successful and for five or six years they did not try it again. Then they gave a morning performance of *Sweethearts*, a play written by W. S. Gilbert, so that Sothern might see it. On this occasion the theatre was crowded and, thus encouraged, they gave several afternoon performances of *Peril* in the following year. Then in 1878 they gave regular matinées of *Diplomacy*.

Bancroft combined the sure instinct of the born moneymaker with the genuine humanity of the reformer. He never feared to invest money in order to make it and he was lavish for those days, not only in the dressing of his plays, but in the treatment of his company. He disliked the old 'benefit' system by which actors were forced to chance their arm for a proportion of their salary, and from the first he paid a living wage, increasing salaries as soon as success made this possible. As examples of the changes during twenty years' management, he tells us that an actor named George Honey was paid £60 a week to play a part in a revival of *Caste* for which four years before he had received £18 a week, while when Mrs Stirling played in the final revival of that comedy, she got eight times the salary paid to the actress who first played her part.

As a young man Bancroft had been very much mortified by the system by which actors were paid. Everyone in the theatre, from cleaners and dressers to the principal actors, had to assemble on Saturday mornings outside the treasury to receive their pay. His first act when he came into management was to institute the custom by which the salary of an actor was delivered to him in his dressing room.

He tells us that he thinks the most valuable quality in the management of a theatre is courage, and he adds that he is speaking chiefly in respect of the strength of will necessary to withdraw a play while it is still remunerative, so that it becomes part of the repertory of the theatre and may be revived when the time is ripe or used as a stop-gap in the event of the failure of some other play. It was largely this policy that accounted for the financial success of the Bancroft management. On the few occasions when one of their productions was a failure it was withdrawn immediately and when they were at a loss for a new production they used one of the Robertson comedies as a stop-gap.

The dramatic critics seemed to feel then, as many do now, that managements had a moral duty to find new plays by English writers even at some cost to themselves, and although the Bancrofts did not share this feeling, they, like other managements, would have welcomed the opportunity to put on a new play by a writer of talent. It was a sign of the times that after Robertson's early death in 1871 and after 'long and well-weighed consideration', they decided that the first successor to the Robertson comedies should be Lord Lytton's *Money*. 'They looked about them for an "original" English comedy, and it is certainly not their fault if they found nothing fresher nor weightier than this poor artificial *Money*, covered with the dust of a hundred prompters' boxes, and faded with the glare of a thousand footlights.'[3]

Money, to the modern reader more 'infantile' than any of Robertson's plays, gave the Bancrofts their most successful season, with the one exception of the year they prdouced

[3] Henry James, *The Scenic Art*, p. 149. In fact James wrote this about the later production of *Money* at the Haymarket.

School. During the next thirteen years of their management they occasionally produced a new English play, notably *Man and Wife* by Wilkie Collins and *Sweethearts* by W. S. Gilbert, but apart from the constantly revived Robertson comedies they were dependent in the main on new productions of old plays or adaptations from the French.

Of the revivals the two most notable at the Prince of Wales's Theatre were *The School for Scandal* (1874) and *The Merchant of Venice* (1875). In the production of these plays the Bancrofts reached the high point of their particular style. The staging and dressing of the former involved many visits to the British Museum and also to Knole House, 'there to choose such types of rooms as, from their wealth of pictures and old furniture, might serve the purpose best'. In Lady Sneerwell's drawing-room amber curtains were drawn back from quilted panels of gold satin, and Lady Sneerwell in powder and brocade sat in a high marquetry chair drinking tea out of real china. At Sir Peter Teazle's a real chandelier suspended by a crimson silken cord lit tapestries on the semi-circular walls. In Charles Surface's room the genuine Turkish carpet was of thick pile, the bookcases were of oak and the books bound in russia leather. Lady Teazle in powder, satin and diamonds was followed at Lady Sneerwell's by a page who was a real Negro and who lived in Mrs Bancroft's house during the run of the piece. The minuet was danced at Lady Sneerwell's reception for the first time, although it has since been so often repeated as to be believed part of the original work.

The Merchant of Venice was one of the most famous failures in theatrical history. During the preparations for its production Mrs Bancroft paid a call on a young actress named Ellen Terry who, known to the public as a child, had then disappeared into seclusion with her lover E. W. Godwin the architect, but had recently returned to London bringing with her the two illegitimate children who were to become known as Edward Gordon Craig and Edith Craig. Mrs Bancroft asked Ellen Terry to play Portia in the coming production, and she added that she and her husband hoped also to employ Godwin in the capacity of archaeological supervisor of the production design. 'My work,' Ellen Terry wrote to the Bancrofts, 'will, I feel certain, be *joyful* work, and joyful work *should* turn out *good* work.'

The Bancrofts travelled to Venice with their principal scene painter and his assistant, where drawings were made from which the scenery and drop curtains were designed. Neither trouble nor money was spared, but, in spite of the beauty and authenticity of the costumes, the production was a failure, although a memorable one. Squire Bancroft wrote:

It all looked so unlike a theatre and so much more like old Italian pictures than anything that had previously been shown upon the stage. Some of the dresses seemed to puzzle many among the audience, notably those worn by Bassanio and the Venetian nobles, who accompanied him to Belmont in their velvet robes of state, the gorgeous attendants on the Prince of Morocco; and the Spaniards who accompanied the Prince of Aragon. It may be that it all came a little before the proper time, and that we saw things too far in advance. . . . I account it a failure to be proud of.

But probably the real reason for the failure was Charles Coghlan's performance as Shylock. Bancroft said that the extent of his failure was a mystery and that he was so undecided how to play the part that on the night of the first performance he lingered on the staircase and then went back to his dressing-room and tore off his wig and make-up. And Ellen Terry said: 'Coghlan's Shylock was not even bad. It was *nothing.*'

However, the audiences, if small, were distinguished. Ellen Terry wrote that 'a poetic and artistic atmosphere pervaded the front of the house as well as the stage itself', while a member of the audience wrote of her: 'Imagine never having seen Ellen Terry, expecting nothing, and having her sprung upon you in the heyday of her youth and beauty and exquisite art!'

The paucity of English dramatists forced the Bancrofts to do as the rest of London did, after Robertson's death, and produce adapatations from the French. Victorien Sardou was the most popular playwright of his time and wrote many plays for Sarah Bernhardt. He had great dramatic power and was a brilliant craftsman, excelling in what is known as the 'well-made' play. His characters, it has been said, lack only life. At this time a school of writers was arising who regarded the 'well-made' play with contempt and Shaw spoke of 'Sardoodledum'. Yet, except where genius is present, a more successful formula is seldom found. The music of Puccini has preserved for us an example of

Sardou's work and, now that the bloom of the contemporary is off, the well-contrived melodrama of *Tosca* seems to many people to wear better than the pseudo-philosophic verbiage of most of Shaw's plays. Squire Bancroft had suffered on more than one occasion from playwrights who delivered two excellent acts and then a weak third, and he did not despite the well-made play. After the failure of a new play by H. J. Byron, he commissioned an adaptation of Sardou's *Nos Intimes* from a writer named B. C. Stephenson, who wrote under the name of Bolton Rowe, Clement Scott, the dramatic critic, was brought into collaboration with Stephenson, taking for the purpose the name of Saville Rowe. *Nos Intimes* was done at the Prince of Wales's in 1876 as *Peril* and, with the Kendals in the company, was extremely successful. Following this Bancroft went to Paris to see Sardou's new play *Dora* and, after the scene for three men, for which *Dora* became famous, he bought the English rights without waiting for the end. *Dora*, in adaptation again by Bolton and Saville Rowe and re-named *Diplomacy*, became one of the most successful of all the Bancroft plays and indeed of the plays of this period. It was revived as late as 1913 by Gerald du Maurier with Gladys Cooper, in 1924 by Gladys Cooper and in 1932 by du Maurier once more. Later at the Haymarket Bancroft gave the first London production to *Fedora*, another of Sardou's plays to become part of the English repertory, a famous production of it being given by Beerbohm Tree with Mrs Patrick Campbell.

When we come to consider the enormous fortune that Squire Bancroft made it is interesting to speculate how much of it would have gone to his authors had there been a royalty system. Tom Robertson was simply on the salary list of the Prince of Wales's Theatre, while the English rights in *Diplomacy* were acquired for the initial purchase price of £1,500 – at that time by far the largest sum ever paid for a foreign play.

Many famous actors and actresses played with the Bancrofts at the Prince of Wales's Theatre. Those that are remembered today include Johnston Forbes-Robertson, William Terriss, Albert Chevalier, Ellen and Marion Terry. But the actor who contributed most to the success of the Bancroft company and the Robertson comedies was John Hare, who joined the Prince of Wales's company almost at the beginning, and who played in all six Robertson comedies and Sir Peter Teazle in *The School for Scandal*. His gift for comedy was so great that he made his own name, while contributing to the success of *Society*, merely by going to sleep.

Hare was a close friend of the Bancrofts and their good relationship was maintained although he became a rival. After playing in *The School for Scandal* Hare left the Prince of Wales's Theatre and went into management himself at the Court. For several years the companies at these two small theatres presented London with a choice of comedy, because Hare took with him the acting style and the scenic innovations developed in the productions of the Robertson comedies. Squire Bancroft, believing there was room for two comedy theatres, did not fear the rivalry of his friend and indeed went out of his way to help him.

Then in 1879 Bancroft was offered the lease of the St James's Theatre which had lately been bought by Lord Kilmorey. He refused the offer, partly because he felt no particular need to leave the Prince of Wales's at that time and partly because the Haymarket Theatre, the London theatre most beloved of actors, had lately been through a period of bad luck and he believed it might become available. A week or two later he heard that John Hare had acquired the lease of the St James's in partnership with the Kendals. 'The amicable rivalry of our old friend Hare [Bancroft writes] at another small outlying theatre, as the Court was, had mattered little – indeed, was often good for both of us – but this news mattered much. So powerful a trio as himself with the Kendals, in a new and better-placed house, rendered handsome and up-to-date, "gave me pause". It was a supreme moment to search for the possibility of saying "check"! '

Less than twenty-four hours after he heard the news Bancroft was shown into the office of J. S. Clarke, the lessee of the Haymarket Theatre, a man he had never met. 'I am going to put my cards at once on the table,' he said. 'I want the Haymarket Theatre: what do you want for it?'

Bancroft's sense of an opportunity was not mistaken, and a few days later the remainder of Clarke's lease was assigned to him together with a new lease for a further period of ten years – the period he already believed should be long enough to make his fortune.

Bancroft acquired the Haymarket for an annual figure which did not exceed £5,000 including rates and insurance, but he pledged himself to spend £10,000 on it. In fact, he spent £17,000 before the curtain rose on his first production and a total of £20,000 altogether. The whole of the auditorium of the famous theatre was pulled down and re-built, and in the new auditorium the pit was abolished. Originally the pit had occupied the entire ground floor of London theatres, the richer classes being seated in the dress circle and private boxes. Gradually the modern stall was introduced and, row by row, in Bancroft's words, the cushioned chairs encroached upon the narrow benches, until at last in many theatres all that was left of the old-fashioned pit was a low ceilinged cavern hidden away under the dress circle. Bancroft was the first to do away with the pit altogether and to put the cheaper seats entirely in the upper parts of the house. The pit remained in many London theatres well into the twentieth century.

On the night when the curtain rose for the first time on the new Haymarket theatre it did so to howls and hooting and angry cries of 'Where's the pit?' which, with the OP riots graven deep in theatrical memory, must have been a singularly terrifying circumstance. And indeed when Bancroft walked on to the stage it was twenty minutes before peace was restored. But the disapproval of the audience on this occasion was only partial, since the occupants of the stalls applauded violently as long as the cheaper parts kept the uproar going, and the popularity of the manager and his wife was so great and the desire of the whole audience to see the play so urgent that, once the demonstration had been made, the protest died and the abolition of the pit became an accepted fact.

Here is a description of the new Haymarket by Henry James;

Mr. Bancroft has transformed the Haymarket—which was an antiquated and uncomfortable house with honourable traditions, which had latterly declined – into the perfection of a place of entertainment. Brilliant, luxuriant, softly cushioned and perfectly aired, it is almost entertainment enough to sit there and admire the excellent device by which the old-fashioned and awkward

proscenium has been suppressed and the stage set all around in
an immense gilded frame, like that of some magnificent picture.
Within this frame the stage, with everything that is upon it, glows
with a radiance that seems the very atmosphere of comedy.[4]

James could not, however, refrain from some gloomy head-
shaking over the prospects of the venture.

The Haymarket has gained by being taken by Mr. and Mrs.
Bancroft, but we are not sure that this humorous couple have
bettered themselves with the public by leaving the diminutive
playhouse to which they taught the public the road. The Prince
of Wales's is a little theatre and the pieces produced there dealt
mainly in little things – presupposing a great many chairs and
tables, carpets, curtains, and knicknacks, and an audience placed
close to the stage. They might, for the most part, have been written
by a cleverish visitor at a country-house, and acted in the drawing-
room by his fellow inmates. The comedies of the late Mr. Robertson
were of this number, and these are certainly among the most
diminutive experiments ever attempted in the drama. It is among
the habits formed upon Mr. Robertson's pieces that the company
of the Prince of Wales's have grown up, and it is possible that they
may not have all the success they desire in accommodating themselves to a larger theatre.

The success of the Bancroft management at the Haymarket
has no parallel in theatrical history. Irving said later: ' "B" is
the only actor since Garrick who made a fortune purely by
management of his own theatre – I mean without the aid of
provincial tours or visits to America.'

Opening with a revival of *Money*, which to his surprise quite
quickly made a profit of £5,000, Bancroft followed with a
revival of the 'diminutive' *School*, which made £10,000 in the
same season. He learned from this that in the larger theatre big
money could be made during the early part of the run of a
piece when the house was sold out. He adopted a policy of
short runs mainly of revivals of the repertory he had built up
at the Prince of Wales's Theatre. He put on *Money*, *Masks and
Faces*, *The School for Scandal*, *Diplomacy*, and the Robertson
comedies *School*, *Ours*, *Society* and *Caste*.

[4] Since praise from this critic was so hardly won it is worth recording that in a
different context he wrote: 'The company at the Prince of Wales's play with a finish,
a sense of detail, what the French call *ensemble*, and a general good grace,' which deserve
explicit recognition.'

The policy of revivals was more or less forced upon him. He continually sought new plays but he found very few. During his years at the Haymarket he put on a new play by Arthur Pinero, *Lords and Commons*, and two adaptations from the French of Victorien Sardou, *Odette* and *Fedora*.

As time went on Bancroft had more and more difficulty in casting plays because of competition from the ever increasing rival managements. One notable addition to his company came to him unsought. He received one day a visit from Mrs Labouchere, the wife of the Liberal politician and journalist, who acted under her professional name of Henrietta Hodson. She told him that Mrs Langtry, the Jersey Lily, had determined to go upon the stage and was to make her debut at an afternoon performance for the Royal General Theatrical Fund as Miss Hardcastle in *She Stoops to Conquer*. Mrs Labouchere had come to ask if she might have the use of the Haymarket Theatre for this purpose. Reflecting that the history of Mrs Langtry's extraordinary career disposed of any fear that she might fail through the ordeal of 'facing the public', and knowing that if he refused her his theatre she would not have far to seek another, Bancroft agreed immediately. It is well known that Mrs Langtry had a long and successful career on the stage. Her first professional part, following the success of her matinée, was Blanche Hay in a revival of *Ours*.

In general, however, the casting of plays became an ever-increasing worry and one cannot help wondering whether Bancroft, having in so short a time so thoroughly put all the old comedies to work, did not also begin to ask himself how long he could go on using *Society* or *School* or *Caste* as a stop-gap for new plays that failed to materialise. Neither of these things might have weighed very strongly with him, however, but for a third and totally unexpected development. He had confidently assumed that it would be possible to make a fortune at the Haymarket in ten years or so. After four years had passed he found he had already done this.

He began to look about him for some means of easing the burden of management and achieving some leisure to enjoy the riches that were his. At first he considered taking a partner and he boldly suggested to Hare that he should give up the St

James's Theatre and, bringing the Kendals with him, join his wife and himself at the Haymarket.

Roughly the proposition was that he and they should give up that theatre and join forces with us – as partners – at the Haymarket, my idea being that the combined strength of our five names would be unassailable; that the theatre, like the Comédie Française, should rarely be closed; that three of the names at the least should always be in the programme, and the whole five of them for a considerable part of the year.

But here he met with a refusal.

The project did not proceed far enough with Hare for me to go into figures; and those dreadful things, very likely, seemed to him an insurmountable objection. The large profits made by us at the Haymarket were, I think, as little suspected as known; and, naturally enough, at the first glance it may have seemed impossible that they could have borne such division as I proposed. Or it may be that what was really strength looked like weakness. At any rate, our old friend decided against my proposal.

So, having failed to divide the work of managing the theatre, Bancroft, aged forty-four, his wife two years older, calmly decided to give it up altogether. In 1885, twenty years after Marie Wilton opened at the Prince of Wales's Theatre, Mr and Mrs Bancroft retired with a fortune. They owed a great deal of their phenomenal success to a willingness to risk money in order to make money; much, too, to their excellent judgment of plays and willingness to cut the loss on any mistake they made (at the Haymarket they made none, although on more than one occasion they decided against plays they had intended to produce after hearing them read). How extraordinarily shrewd was their general conduct in management is revealed by the fact that it was possible for John Hare, at the St James's Theatre round the corner, following the same policies, with the Kendals in his company, not to 'suspect' the profits that were being made at the Haymarket.

Marie Bancroft lived to be 82, Squire Bancroft to be 85. Ellen Terry was to write of them:

The brilliant story of the Bancroft management of the Old Prince of Wales's Theatre used to be more familiar twenty years back than it is now. I think that few of the present generation of play-goers who point out on the first night of important productions a remarkably striking figure of a man with erect carriage, white hair, and flashing, dark eyes – a man whose eyeglass, manners and clothes all suggest Thackeray and Major Pendennis, in spite of his success in keeping abreast of everything modern—few play-goers, I say, who point this man out as Sir Squire Bancroft could give any account of what he and his wife did for the English theatre. Nor do the public who see an elegant little lady starting for a drive from a certain house in Berkeley Square realise that this is Marie Wilton, afterwards Mrs. Bancroft, now Lady Bancroft, the comedian who created the heroines of Tom Robertson.

And she added:

I have never, even in Paris, seen anything more admirable than the *ensemble* of the Bancroft productions. Every part in the domestic comedies the presentation of which they made their policy, was played with such point and finish that the more rough, uneven, and emotional acting of the present day has not produced anything so good in the same line.

And fifteen years after this was written, Frederick Lonsdale (who in some respects might be regarded as in the direct succession from Tom Robertson) could still describe Lady Bancroft as an 'inimitable' raconteur, while she could still cast spells on his children by telling them stories of her youth and the repeated omens of her good fortune.

During all the long years of their retirement the Bancrofts re-appeared seldom on the stage. In 1893 they acted together in a revival by John Hare of *Diplomacy* at the Garrick Theatre in a cast which included Forbes-Robertson and Olga Nethersole, and in the following year Lady Bancroft appeared as Lady Franklin under the same management in *Money*. In 1895 at the Haymarket Theatre she appeared with Herbert Beerbohm Tree and Mrs Patrick Campbell in a revival of *Fedora*. These seem to have been her only professional appearances during the whole period with the exception of single performances. In 1889 Bancroft made a notable appearance at the Lyceum Theatre with Sir Henry Irving in a play called *The Dead Heart*. In this play there is a duel between the characters played by Bancroft and Irving. Both men were short-sighted and at all rehearsals Irving wore his pince-nez and Bancroft his eyeglass, but on the first night these were necessarily abandoned. Here is Bancroft's account of it.

From all I have heard said of it the fight must have been very well done – real, brief and determined. It was a grim business, in the sombre moonlit room, and certainly gave the impression that one of the two combatants would not leave it alive. The scene remains in the memory, and I often still hear from many old play-goers that it was the best thing of the kind they ever saw.

And Bancroft adds in a book written after Irving's death, that he refrained from asking Irving, as William Terriss had done when rehearsing a similar scene in *The Corsican Brothers*, whether some of the moonlight might fall on him, as 'nature is impartial'.[5]

Bancroft had another characteristic in common with Irving – the zest with which he played the part of actor-manager. Although he is known for his wise and benevolent management and for the innovations for which he was responsible rather than for the exceptional quality of his talents, it must not be thought that he neglected his opportunities to pay tribute in his personal behaviour to the profession in which he stood so high. Marguerite Steen has given us the following description of the two men. 'Irving swaggered about the town with long hair, a "wide-awake", and a fur collared overcoat; Bancroft swaggered about with a top-hat, an eyeglass and a cane. Neither of them ever ceased acting, on the stage or off. In days before "publicity" was commercialised, each was his own best publicity agent.'

For nearly forty years Squire Bancroft and his wife lived the life of the rich and leisured classes. They liked travel and they had a taste for pictures and furniture. They had one son, George, who wrote *The Ware Case* and a new adaptation of *Diplomacy* for Gerald du Maurier's production of 1913. Bancroft raised many thousands of pounds for hospitals when he emerged from his retirement to travel round England giving readings of *A Christmas Carol*. In 1897 he was knighted for the services rendered to the theatre by himself and his wife.

[5] Terriss, William, 1847–97. One of the few actors who was openly unafraid of Henry Irving. He was assassinated on his way into the Adelphi Theatre in 1897.

Sir Henry Irving
1838-1905

Henry Irving once said that Edmund Kean's reputation was a posthumous one. 'If you read the newspapers of the time you will find that during his acting days he was terribly mauled.' And he added that Garrick's impersonations were not much written about in his lifetime.

The point he wished to emphasise was that he himself might expect a 'posthumous reputation'. He found it necessary to do this because at no time in his career was there general agreement about the quality of his acting. William Archer[1] said of him:

There has probably never been an actor of equal prominence whose talent, nay whose mere competence has been so much contested. He is the idol of a select circle of devotees but even it is small, and its fervour is apt to be tempered with apology. . . . In no single part has general consent pronounced him ideal; in many it has emphatically pronounced him quite the reverse, though the Lyceum was nonetheless crowded on that account.

And Henry James said the same thing in a different way.

Mr Irving's critics may, I suppose, be divided into three categories: those who justify him in whatever he attempts, and consider him an artist of unprecedented brilliancy: those who hold that he did very well in melodrama, but that he flies too high when he attempts Shakespeare; and those who, in vulgar parlance, can see nothing in him at all.

---

[1] Archer, William, 1856–1924. One of the leading dramatic critics of the late nineteenth century. Wrote in *Figaro*, the *World*, the *Tribunal* and the *Nation*. Translated Ibsen's plays and edited his collected works. Author of many books on the theatre and a play called *The Green Goddess*. In 1877, as a young man in Edinburgh, he was joint author

Today we must still attempt to reach a decision on the matter in spite of the conflicting evidence, because Henry Irving's claim on our attention is that he was one of the greatest actors in our history. The Bancrofts' pretensions were of a much smaller kind. Honest perfectionists, modestly intent on fame and fortune, they happened to launch a revolution in theatrical style and customs. Irving gave his whole life to his art and he would not wish to be remembered except by the quality of his contribution to it.

It is not of course true that his circle was small or apologetic. As to the first, Archer contradicts himself immediately in the sentence 'the Lyceum was nonetheless crowded on that account', and anyone who has read Edward Gordon Craig on Irving, or Joseph Hatton, or Ellen Terry, or any of a dozen others, will know that it was not apologetic. Gordon Craig opens his book *Henry Irving* by saying: 'Let me state at once, in clearest unmistakable terms, that I have never known of, or seen, or heard, a greater actor than was Irving.' Yet in order to understand the extent and vigour of the controversy one has only to turn again to Henry James.

That an actor so handicapped, as they say in London, by nature and culture should have enjoyed such prosperity is a striking proof of the absence of a standard, of the chaotic condition of taste. Mr Irving's Macbeth, which I saw more than a year ago and view under the mitigations of time, was not pronounced one of his great successes; but it was acted, nevertheless, for many months, and it does not appear to have injured his reputation. Passing through London, and curious to make the acquaintance of the great English actor of the day, I went with alacrity to see it; but my alacrity was more than equalled by the vivacity of my disappointment. I sat through the performance in a sort of melancholy amazement. There are barren failures and there are interesting failures, and this performance seemed to me to deserve the less complimentary of these classifications. It inspired me, however, with no ill-will toward the artist, for it must be said of Mr. Irving

---

with Robert Lowe and George Halkett of a pamphlet called *The Fashionable Tragedian* which deplored Irving's popularity, claiming that his diction was execrable, his mannerisms grotesque and his scholarship a pretence. Later Archer developed a greater admiration for Irving and attempted an impartial analysis of his acting in *Henry Irving, Actor and Manager: A Critical Study*, from which the quotations in the following pages are taken.

that his aberrations are not of a vulgar quality, and that one likes him, somehow, in spite of them. But one's liking takes the form of making one wish that really he had selected some other profession than the histrionic. Nature has done very little to make an actor of him. His face is not dramatic; it is the face of a sedentary man, a clergyman, a lawyer, an author, an amiable gentleman – of anything other than a possible Hamlet or Othello. His figure is of the same cast, and his voice completes the want of illusion. His voice is apparently wholly unavailable for purposes of declamation. To say that he speaks badly is to go too far; to my sense he simply does not speak at all—in any way that, in an actor, can be called speaking. He does not pretend to declaim or dream of declaiming. Shakespeare's finest lines pass from his lips without his paying the scantiest tribute to their quality. Of what the French call *diction* – of the art of delivery – he has apparently not a suspicion. This forms three-fourths of an actor's obligations and in Mr. Irving's acting these three-fourths are simply cancelled. What is left to him with the remaining fourth is to be 'picturesque'; and this even his partisans admit he has made his speciality. This concession darkens Mr. Irving's prospects as a Shakespearean actor. You can play hop-scotch on one foot, but you cannot cut with one blade of a pair of scissors, and you cannot play Shakespeare by being simply picturesque.

Henry James means more to us today than Gordon Craig, and the tendency would be to identify ourselves with him except for one thing – he goes too far. In the first place he condemns the taste of a whole generation of playgoers as well as Henry Irving and, secondly, he would have us believe that this actor had the face of 'a sedentary man', an amiable gentleman'. The first charge is so extreme it arouses curiosity, the second comes into conflict with one of the few pieces of evidence we have by which we may judge for ourselves. We know from photographs what Irving looked like and may decide for ourselves whether he had the face of an amiable, sedentary man.

One of the most famous of all descriptions of acting is Gordon Craig's description of Irving in *The Bells*. He begins by telling us that one of the characters on the stage has just mentioned the night, many years ago, when the Polish Jew was murdered. Then he goes on:

Irving was buckling his second shoe, seated, and leaning over it with his two long hands stretched down over the buckles. We suddenly saw these fingers stop their work; the crown of the head suddenly seemed to glitter and become frozen – and then, at the pace of the slowest and most terrified snail, the two hands, still motionless and dead, were seen to be coming up the side of the leg. . . . the whole torso of the man, also seeming frozen, was gradually, and by an almost imperceptible movement, seen to be drawing up and back, as it would straighten a little and to lean a little against the back of the chair on which he was seated.

Once in that position – motionless – eyes fixed ahead of him and fixed on us all – there he sat for the space of ten to twelve seconds, which I can assure you seemed to us all like a lifetime, and then said – and said in a voice deep and overwhelmingly beautiful 'Oh, you were talking of that – were you?' And as the last syllable was uttered, there came afar off the regular throbbing sound of the sledge-bells. . . .

He moves his head slowly from us – the eyes still somehow with us – and moves it to the right – taking as long as a long journey to discover a truth takes. He looks to the faces on the right – nothing. Slowly the head revolves back again, down, and along the tunnels of thought and sorrow, and at the end the face and eyes are bent upon those to the left of him . . . utter stillness . . . nothing there either. . . .

The difficulty however with detailed descriptions of acting is that they tell us what was done but not how it was done and this kind of thing – 'taking as long as a long journey to discover a truth takes' – requires a preliminary faith if we are to be sure of anything more than that Irving's method was a slow one. Here, for instance, is Shaw's description of Irving in *A Story of Waterloo* to put beside it.

A squeak is heard behind the scenes: it is the childish treble that once rang like a trumpet on the powder-waggon at Waterloo, Enter Mr. Irving, in a dirty white wig, toothless, blear-eyed, palsied, shaky at the knees, stooping at the shoulders, incredibly aged and very poor, but respectable. He makes his way to his chair, and can only sit down, so stiff are his aged limbs, very slowly and creakily. . . . The corporal cannot recognise his grandniece at first, when he does, he asks her questions about children – children who have long gone to their graves at ripe ages. She prepares his tea, he sups it noisily and ineptly, like an infant. . . . He gets a bronchial attack and gasps for paregoric. . . . He rises more creakily than before, but with his faithful grandniece's arm fondly supporting him. He dodders across the stage, expressing a hope that the flies will not be too 'owdacius', and sits down on another chair with his joints crying more loudly than ever for some of the oil of youth. We feel that we could watch him sitting down for ever.

It is clear that in this second passage Shaw is guying Irving, but he does also show how meaningless is any direct attempt to reveal an actor's art by a narrative description of it. In both these passages the miming might be of the highest quality or that of an old ham in a Victorian melodrama; it might hold us entranced or reduce us to giggles.

One of the strangest aspects of the accounts of Irving is that even where they relate to matters of fact an extremity of statement on one side does nothing to prohibit an equal extremity on the other. Gordon Craig, for instance, tells us that Irving could 'bring the house down.'

I think it has not been your fortune to hear what is called 'the house coming down'. Even in the epoch of Irving it was seldom that anyone else 'brought the house down' – but Irving 'brought it down'.

A terrific sweep of applause is not 'bringing the house down'. 'Bringing the house down' is when everybody simultaneously calls out and applauds simultaneously and electrically. . . . You have been to the Russian Ballet perhaps on one of its great nights, or you have heard Chaliapine's reception at Covent Garden. Well, that is not what I mean either. Those are ovations, but mild ovations. The thing I mean had three times the capacity.

Music-lovers will find this a very extreme statement but it does nothing to prevent the following. 'The crowded audiences at the Lyceum as a rule applaud but feebly and the attendants in the front of the house are not above contributing to the rapturous ovation. . . . The true explanation is that the majority of the audience are intellectually interested not emotionally excited.' In the second of these sentences William Archer contradicts almost every other account of Irving's acting. Irving gave much thought to his interpretations of the major roles and particularly in Shakespeare often forsook the traditional readings, but his contemporaries speak again and again of his almost mesmeric hold over the emotions of his audiences, of his power to inspire fear and communicate his own excessive guilt.

It is clearly impossible to arrive at an opinion of the quality of Irving's acting by the method of balancing one man's words against another's, and we must look for some more positive means to judge it. Two things must prejudice us heavily towards the view that Irving is to be ranked among the great actors of all time. The first concerns the composition of the 'select' circle which Archer says 'idolised' Irving. In this circle, apparently uninterested in the controversy and the criticisms, certainly not tempering fervour with apology, was the whole of the acting profession.

Irving arrived in London in 1867, an almost unknown actor from the provinces. Four or five years later he was the acknowledged head of his profession, a position he retained until his death in 1905. This supremacy was awarded him without strife. Actors idolised him and fell in behind him with unreserved loyalty and devotion. It is difficult to find a theatrical biography of the time in which Irving's quality is questioned or his right to the position of leader challenged, either by the subject or the author of the book. Squire Bancroft was in management for six years before Irving took over the Lyceum, but, when he speaks of Irving, he does so with an assumption that it was natural to pay him homage, telling little stories that have no point other than that Irving called on his wife and himself late one evening, or spoke kind words to their son. The list of actors who regarded him as the 'Chief' or the 'Guvnor' includes the most famous of the day in spite of the fact that the Lyceum productions were designed round himself and Ellen Terry and that he gave no quarter to young and aspiring performers. The list of books in which he is spoken of in that peculiarly Victorian tone of reverent sentimentality usually reserved for the Queen is as long as the list of actors. From Ellen Terry herself and her son Edward Gordon Craig, who, if not a remarkable actor was an innovator and a man of great talent, through William Terriss, Sir Arthur Pinero, Sir Johnston Forbes-Robertson and Sir George Alexander to Sir John Martin Harvey, his devoted personal circle included the leading names of the day, while outside the Lyceum Company he was accorded the same measure of respect as within it.

Irving might have been regarded by the actors of today as the old, ham actor who played in Victorian melodrama, but he is not. No intervening generation has queried his unique talent.

'Do as the great Irving did,' Gerald du Maurier remarked, instructing a young actor on some particular point. And as witness for our own day we have the greatest of them all. In a recent series of televised interviews with actors, Kenneth Tynan asked Sir Laurence Olivier about his performance of Richard II and Sir Laurence replied: 'First of all I had heard imitations of old actors imitating Henry Irving; and so I did, right away, an imitation of these old actors imitating Henry Irving's voice – that's why I took a rather narrow kind of vocal address.' And in the same series of interviews Sir John Gielgud talking about his first performance of Hamlet said: 'Of course, Irving was my god, although I'd never seen him; I'd just read about him being Ellen Terry's partner. But the whole idea of this magnetic, strange man, whom I knew I could never be anything like, somehow appealed to me more than any past actor that I'd ever read about. I didn't try to copy, I only took note of all the things he'd done and looked at the pictures of him and so on.'

Why, then, if in the theatre itself recognition of the greatness of Henry Irving is implicit in everything that is said of him, did so great a controversy wage outside it? Sir Laurence Olivier supplies the clue.

As an actor Sir Henry Irving had great faults. First of all there was this narrow, almost nasal kind of vocal address Sir Laurence speaks of, secondly there was his strange manner of pronouncing the English language, and thirdly there was, according to some accounts, an almost grotesque method of moving about the stage. Sir Henry, we are told, said 'Gud' for 'God', 'Cut-thrut dug', 'Tak the rup frum mey nek', 'Ritz' for 'rich', 'seyt' for 'sight', 'stod' for 'stood', 'hond' or 'hend' for 'hand', while for 'To trammel up the consequence', he said 'tram-mele up-p the cunsequence'. And, while so hideously distorting the language, he moved about the stage with depressed head, and protruding shoulders, making with his legs sidelong and backward skirmishes.

In Irving's day there were no schools of acting, no repertory theatres. There were the provincial theatres and the old stock companies where a young man might learn from the old stock actors how to play stock characters and for the rest might teach himself. As Irving painfully acquired a technique with which to express his natural talent, he could neither see nor hear himself. Faults that today would be corrected during his early training became a part of his personality. 'Do I say Gud when I say Gud?' he once asked.[2]

How, then was it possible for Gordon Craig to say: 'I have never known of, or seen, or heard a greater actor than was Irving'? The answer, of course, is that to be great is not to be faultless but to be great. It speaks for Irving's superb quality that it could transcend his absurd diction and his grotesque walk. The crime that those who write critically for money are always in danger of committing is not to fail in the detection of faults but to fail to recognise genius when it appears unheralded.

In Irving's case the trouble was not that his great talents went unsung but that they were so trumpeted that anyone, hurrying to experience for the first time the impact of his acting and confronted with a thinnish voice, a strange diction and some odd mannerisms, was apt to be so engrossed and repelled by these as to be incapable of perceiving his merits. To take a further example from opera, it sometimes happens that a singer has one or two notes that are so ugly that people who know her only by reputation are on first acquaintance shocked out of critical judgment and musical appreciation.

'Is that what all the fuss is about?' they ask, and only on closer acquaintance fall victim to the general artistry of a whole performance. Archer says of Irving:

The taste for his art must be acquired, and the mere commencement of the process is so irksome that they [his critics] never get beyond the first sip, as it were, but make a wry face and refuse to repeat the dose. Familiarity with Mr. Irving's art, so far from lessening respect, may almost be called a necessary condition of the merest tolerance.

And:

At first I did not like it at all, but little by little, I found my nerves adjust themselves to the inevitable. My attention was no

---

[2] In an earlier generation Leigh Hunt complains bitterly of John Philip Kemble's pronunciation, of which he gives the following examples: aitches=aches; bird=beard; churful=cheerful; conshince=conscience; airth=earth; air=err; farwell=farewell; furful=fearful. And in our own day we have a leading politician who adopts the airth= earth vowel sound.

longer absorbed in making the phonetic changes necessary to trans-
mute Mr. Irving's speech into English, or wondering where his
limbs were going to carry him next.

Then an anonymous critic in *The Evening Transcript* writing
of Irving's performance in *Hamlet* said:

He delivers long speeches in a curious monotone as to pitch; he
cuts up sentences into disjointed bits with apparently little reference to the meaning, taking breath, as one would say of a singer,
in most adventurous places. Yet, with these indubitably grave
faults, he manages by some magic to get the full meaning out of
almost every sentence, and the emphasis falls upon the right word;
one finds little or nothing of that over-valuing adjectives and the
smaller parts of speech at the expense of nouns and verbs. . . . With
all his peculiarities of speech, the ear is never wounded by a common, cheap or vulgar inflexion. . . . Mr. Irving may have many
ungainly idiosyncrasies of pose and gesture, yet, such is the innate
dignity of the man, that we never find them ludicrous; never was
a man more gracefully awkward.

That passage, apart from what it tells us about Irving, is
valuable as an illustration of the second reason for believing in
his greatness as an actor. There is so much difficulty in re-creat-
ing the splendours of art that when two talents fuse to
accomplish it – as when a talented writer speaks of a talented
actor – the result is convincing. It requires no particular ability
to detect and condemn faults of taste and execution but it
requires truth and skill to communicate what is remarkable in
a performance. Irving's acting was written about by some of
the great literary talents of his day, and, in spite of Henry
James, there are passages that cannot be set aside. One may
discard entirely the views of his henchmen and quote only
from those who were regarded as critical of him, or those of
that happily cynical nature which inspires later generations
with confidence, and we can find more than enough to support
the claim that Irving, like Kean, was worthy of his posthumous
reputation. Bernard Shaw said of him:

Those who understood the art of the theatre and knew his
limitations could challenge him on every point except one; and
that was his eminence. Even to call him eminent belittles his
achievement: he was pre-eminent. He was not pre-eminent in or
for this, that or the other talent or faculty: his pre-eminence was

abstract and positive: a quality in itself and in himself so powerful that it carried him to Westminster Abbey.

And elsewhere:

He was utterly unlike anyone else: he could give importance
and a noble melancholy to any sort of drivel that was put into his
mouth; and it was this melancholy, bound up with an impish
humour, which forced the spectator to single him out as a leading
figure with an inevitability that I never saw again in any other
actor until it rose from Irving's grave in the person of a nameless
cinema actor who afterwards became famous as Charlie Chaplin.

William Archer said of Irving that he possessed in quite
abnormal measure that 'magnetic personality' whose power is
'irresistible and indefinable' and that when he walked on the
stage at his first entrance no special stage-management, no
reception, no reference to the play-bill was needed to assure
even the least initiated spectator that he was the most remarkable man on the stage. He thought there might be better stage
faces than Irving's but few more remarkable.

The high forehead, the marked overhanging but flexible eye-
brows, the dark eyes which can by turns be so penetrating, so
dreamy so sinister and so melancholy, the thin straight nose, the
narrow almost lipless sensitive mouth, the hollow cheeks and
marvellously mobile jaw, combine to form an incomparable
vehicle for the expression of a certain range of emotion.

One of the most illuminating comments was made by Ellen
Terry, who said that she admired Irving for what she termed a
'bizarrerie' in his acting which invited derision and mocking
imitation but which lifted his performance above common
realism. And Max Beerbohm seems to be describing something
of the same quality when he says: 'He had, in acting, a keen
sense of humour – of sardonic, grotesque, fantastic humour. He
had an incomparable power for eeriness – for stirring a dim
sense of mystery; and not less masterly was he in evoking a
sharp sense of horror.' And Beerbohm leaves us in no doubt of
Irving's quality in a passage in which he says that one of the
regrets of his life is that he did not see Irving play Hamlet.

I can imagine the gentleness (with a faint strain of cruelty), the
aloofness, the grace and force of intellect, in virtue of which that

performance must have been a very masterpiece of interpretation. I can imagine, too, the mystery with which Irving must have involved, rightly, the figure of Hamlet, making it loom through the mist mightily, as a world-type, not as a mere individual – making it loom as it loomed in the soul of Shakespeare himself – not merely causing it to strut agreeably, littly, as in the average production.

Irving carried the star system as far as it can be carried. Gordon Craig says that he actually preferred plays that had no real merit because when the playwright has done his work too well the actor is not required to put out his full powers. It was when the play was about to crumble that Irving was at his most prodigious.

Today the theatre has been democratised and the economic circumstances ensure that in the theatre our leading actors play only to a small section of the public whose intellectual appreciation is the highest that has ever been known. The Victorian theatre must not be judged by these standards. It was a theatre of personality, of actors who were expected to fill the theatre almost unaided by their colleagues, or by playwrights, or by any great refinement of taste among their audiences. In an actors' theatre audiences must be held by emotional force.

John Henry Brodribb was born in 1838 in a Somerset village called Keinton Mandeville. He was the son of Samuel Brodribb, himself a travelling salesman but the descendant of several generations of farmers, and his wife Mary Behenna, a Cornish girl and a devout Methodist. In 1842, when the child was four years old, the times being exceedingly bad in Somerset, Samuel and Mary Brodribb moved to Bristol to find more lucrative employment; but Mary, who feared in their straitened circumstances to bring up her child in a town, sent him to Cornwall to her sister, Sarah, married to Isaac Penberthy, in the confidence that there he would enjoy at least the benefits of simple food and fresh air. Johnnie Brodribb lived with his aunt and two cousins until he was ten years old, when, on the death of Isaac Penberthy, his aunt could no longer afford to keep him and he was returned to his parents. Mary Brodribb had sent him away in a spirit of self-sacrifice and it seems to have been accepted by all biographers that her decision was wise.

No-one writing about Irving seems ever to have related this separation from his parents at so early an age to his known characteristics as an actor.

In Cornwall the child, who was sweet-tempered and cheerful, gave cause for worry only by a tendency to play-act. At that time a company of actors travelled from village to village performing in a tent and although, if the young Brodribb visited these, it was in defiance of the Methodist rules of his upbringing, it seems to be established that before the age of ten he had announced his ambition to become an actor, could recite passage after passage from Shakespeare and practise the art of ventriloquism. He took revenge for the children of the whole village on an old woman who had persecuted them with threats of hell-fire by appearing at her bedside, wearing a mask, horns and a tail. However, shortly after his tenth birthday, he somewhat allayed anxiety by falling into an ecstasy during a service and professing his conversion to the religion of his fathers.

As a child John Brodribb suffered from a stammer. When he was returned to his parents, who by now were living in London, he attended the City Commercial School and he was lucky in that the headmaster, Dr Pinches, attached much importance to elocution and took this class himself. Here, for the first time, he was encouraged in his passion for recitation and he worked hard to eradicate his stammer. On one occasion at the end of prize-giving at this school, he was congratulated on his performance by an actor named William Creswick, who was at the time playing Hamlet at the Surrey Theatre, and, taking advantage of the fact of his gentleman's presence on so respectable an occasion, he managed to persuade his mother to allow him to be taken to the theatre. As a result, shortly before his twelfth birthday he went with his father to Sadler's Wells to see Phelps play Hamlet, and here he underwent a second conversion described by his biographer as 'as intense and heartfelt as the first'. Laurence Irving writes: 'The close succession of one emotional crisis upon the other may have imbued his self-dedication to the art of acting with the almost religious idealism which was to govern his attitude towards the principle and practice of his profession.'

In all these circumstances it is not surprising to find John Henry Brodribb, on leaving school at the age of thirteen, sitting on a clerk's stool by day but joining by night in the popular pastime of amateur acting and visiting with other stage-struck clerks a school of elocution run by a Mr Henry Thomas. Mr Thomas was an admirer and friend of Charles J. Matthews, a famous comedian of the time, and Laurence Irving suggests that by encouraging his pupils to adopt, when acting comedy, the jaunty, jerky stride successfully employed by Matthews, he was responsible for Irving's peculiar gait, later to be so much criticised.

Mary Brodribb could not compromise her own stern faith to meet her son's passionate longings because she fervently believed that to become a play-actor was to invite hell-fire. At this time she used to beg the friends her son brought home to do all in their power to dissuade him from going on the stage. She received little help from them but she did receive some backing for her views from an unexpected quarter. John Brodribb had made friends during the course of his many visits to Sadler's Wells with a leading actor in Phelps's company named William Hoskins, and for some time he used to go at eight o'clock every morning to Hoskins's house to receive private tuition in elocution and pantomime. When, in the course of time, Hoskins decided to leave Sadler's Wells and try his luck in Australia, he asked his pupil to accompany him. Brodribb hesitated to adopt so extreme a course, and Hoskins then offered, before leaving, to introduce him to the great Phelps himself. 'Sir,' Samuel Phelps said to him then, 'do not go on the stage; it is an ill-requited profession.'

Finding, however, that the young man could not be put off, he offered him two pounds a week to join his company. This Brodribb refused because he had already considered the matter and believed that he must go through the hard school of the provincial stock companies. Hoskins then gave him a letter of recommendation to a provincial manager named Davis, saying: 'You will go on the stage. When you want an engagement present that letter and you will get one.'

At this time actors were expected to find their own properties, and a young man wishing to go on the stage had somehow to provide himself with wigs, swords, buckles, lace, sham jewellery and so on. When John Brodibb received from an uncle a gift of £100, the moment he had awaited seemed to him to have arrived. He made a large investment in stage properties, including among them three swords – symbols of the romance of life that lay ahead. Then he spent some of his remaining capital in a trial of skill. In response to the great vogue for amateur acting the managers of some small theatres allowed amateurs to pay for the privilege of giving a single per-formance, the importance of the role being graded according to the size of the fee. For the sum of three guineas Brodribb played Romeo at the Soho Theatre. It was for this performance that he first took the name Irving, at this time signing himself J. H. B. Irving but, since for stage purposes he preferred the name Henry, he soon dropped John altogether.

When Hoskins's letter of recommendation to Davis produced the offer of an engagement in the stock company of the new Royal Lyceum theatre at Sunderland, Brodribb had, before becoming Irving, to break the news to his parents. At the age of eighteen he was again and this time permanently separated from his mother, who, having left him at the age of four in pursuit of what she believed to be her duty, now saw him depart without her approval or forgiveness, his dedication to his art being matched by her faith in her religion.

Henry Irving's time as a provincial actor in stock com-panies lasted for ten lean and terrible years. He learned at first hand why Phelps had said: 'It is an ill-requited profession,' and even why Kean had asked: 'Can you starve, cocky?' His life had none of the charmed ease of Bancroft's, who followed the same road at about the same time. Bancroft seems always to have had a large measure of control over a lesser talent, but Irving had to strive for a technical equipment adequate to carry the force of genius. Shaw says: 'When Nature intends anyone to be a highly cultivated artist, she generally forces them on by condemning them to fiendishness or loutishness until they fulfill her intention.' Irving was not a lout but he lacked style, polish and control over the means of expression.

Bancroft says of him, describing a chance meeting when he himself was already in management at the Prince of Wales's Theatre and Irving still a struggling provincial actor:

Irving was a born leader . . . and certainly in his later years would have graced, in manner and aspect, any position in life.

This personal attribute came to him gradually when, as it were, he recreated himself. Truth to tell, in the early part of his career he had none of it. In those distant days there was a strong smack of the country actor in his appearance and a suggestion of a type immortalised by Dickens in Mr. Lenville and Mr. Folair.

During his provincial years Irving became a changed personality. Gordon Craig, and following him Laurence Irving, make much of the metamorphosis of Brodribb into Irving, a pictorial and rather simplified concept, but one which for the ordinary reader adequately emphasises the great changes that occurred as the dedicated, intense youth with the slight impediment to his speech and a sweetness of nature that won him many friends became, over the course of his provincial years, the mysterious, magnetic, slightly bohemian, powerful and secret man who dominated the London theatre. The validity of the Brodribb–Irving dissociation is strengthened by the extent to which, as he built up the equipment through which he at last expressed himself, he also perfected the romantic portrait of the actor-manager.

As he steeled himself against poverty and near-starvation he had certain traumatic experiences. The first of these occurred in Sunderland soon after his first appearance on the professional stage. Having survived performances of *Richelieu*, *The Enchanted Lake* and *The Lady of Lyons*, in which he had only a line or two to speak, he dried up while playing the part of Cleomenes in *The Winter's Tale*, no words coming from his lips when he received his cue. He was forced to rush off the stage to the hisses of the audience. Laurence Irving believes that he did not dry up as a result of stage-fright but because momentarily he could not control the only half-conquered impediment to his speech. In any case he was lucky in that his manager stood by him and two old actors, Sam Johnson and Tom Mead, restored some of his confidence with firm and practical advice. It was then he made the promise later punctiliously kept: 'If ever I rise I shall not forget this.'

But his humiliation was, nevertheless, complete and when he got an offer of an engagement at Edinburgh, he gladly left the scene of his disaster.

In Edinburgh the stock company under the management of the Wyndhams had a high reputation and Irving stayed here for two and a half years, during which time he played over four hundred parts – making a name for himself, among other things, as a low comedian. At the end of this time he received from Augustus Harris Sr the offer of a London engagement which, delighted, he accepted. Before leaving the Wyndhams he performed the part of Claude Melnotte in *The Lady of Lyons* for his benefit performance and then, as his grandson puts it, packing in his hamper 'the scrappy components of four hundred and twenty-eight characters', he left for London, in the reasonable belief that his novitiate had come to an end.

Irving left Edinburgh a well-established juvenile lead, ready for the London stage. By one of those unexplained and inconsequent acts which abound in the history of the theatre, Augustus Harris gave him a part of half a dozen lines in a play called *Ivy Hall*, which was an undistinguished failure, and followed this by casting him as Osric to the Hamlet of a very indifferent provincial actor who was advised by the London press to return to the melodrama from whence he sprang. Disappointed and humiliated, Irving asked and received his release from his contract and arranged to return to the provincial stage. Before doing this he made what his biographer has called 'a demonstration of force to cover his retreat'. In those days public readings of plays or poetry at cheap prices attracted large audiences from among those who would not in the ordinary way enter the theatre. At the Crosby Hall in the City of London Irving gave reading of *The Lady of Lyons* and a second one of Sheridan Knowles' *Virginius*, and attracted recognition of his unusual talent. The critics were in attendance and were generally approving, the audience sobbed at the end of *The Lady of Lyons* and one critic wrote of the 'finer and indefinite something which proved incontestably and instantaneously that the fire of genius is present in the artist'.

Fortified by these opinions, Irving travelled to Dublin, little knowing that there a trap was laid for him in which he was to suffer an experience which, as much as any other single thing, has been held accountable for his development. Henry Webb, the manager of the Queen's Theatre, Dublin, had recently dismissed his juvenile lead, George Vincent, for insubordination. Vincent recruited a gang of hooligans to revenge himself on his manager and indirectly on his successor. Irving made his first appearance in a role Vincent had never played and all passed smoothly, but two nights later his entrance on the stage was the signal for an outburst of savage and derisive yelling and whistling sufficient to bring the play to a standstill. For three weeks this was repeated every time Irving appeared in a part that had previously been played by Vincent.

On almost all the famous occasions in theatrical history that an actor has been given 'the bird' it has been because of a gang organised to protest on the part of someone else rather than the result of a spontaneous outburst of disapproval directed at himself. The fact that the booing and screaming are not inspired by the personality or art of the man who suffers them seems not to diminish the appalling shock that is received or the bitterness which such treatment inspires. In later life Irving held himself apart from audiences, treating them if not with contempt at least with indifference, and this has been regarded as a consequence not only of the years he had to wait for recognition of his talent but also of his experience in Dublin. Gordon Craig writing of this time says:

As later on in life he never accepted the applause he received, so we may suppose that he refused to accept this disapproval. How often have I and those who were in his theatre seen him standing while the applause rained down like a cataract, and he obviously there – bowing so *slightly* to show that he was not only there, but aware: yet *never* accepting the applause – enduring it.

However, Gordon Craig grew up in the shadow of Irving and his attitude to him is always solemn, sometimes idolatrous. There are suggestions that Irving possessed two qualities his biographers occasionally lack – a sense of proportion about himself and a sense of humour. His method of taking calls may have been in consequence of his early experiences; or he may have considered that this gravely aloof treatment of an audience he had previously raised to the heights of emotion was effective.

In 1865, the year Marie Wilton opened at the Prince of Wales's Theatre, Irving terminated an engagement at the Theatre Royal, Manchester, after falling out with the management on a matter of principle. He had now been nine years on the stage and he was probably near the height of his powers.

Yet he was penniless, for weeks at a time unemployed and in debt to his friends. When he found employment it was often with wretched companies and for short periods. He drifted from Manchester to Edinburgh and back, to Bury, from there to Oxford, to Birmingham and from there to Liverpool, where he was left stranded when his company was disbanded, and was forced to travel to the Isle of Man for a three-night engagement with an amateur company. Often nearly starving, his frustration was complete.

Then one day in the summer of 1866 he called at the stage-door of the Prince of Wales's Theatre in Liverpool hoping to hear of work. As he turned away empty-handed, forlorn and despairing, the stage-door-keeper ran after him with a letter he had overlooked. It was from Dion Boucicault[3] and it offered Irving a part in a new play to be produced in Manchester. His long and hard apprenticeship was over.

As Rawdon Scudamore, an unscrupulous villain in *The Two Lives of Mary Leigh*, Irving made the play such an overwhelming success in Manchester that, in spite of a far-fetched plot and poor dialogue, offers were made for it by two London managements.[4] Boucicault closed with Miss Herbert at the St James's Theatre, making a condition, immediately accepted, that Irving should play Rawdon Scudamore.

There is often a particular moment in the lives of great singers and actors when – through a peculiar identification with some particular part or through sympathetic and masterly direction – they miraculously raise their performance on to a new plane. It is doubtful if anything of this sort happened to Irving. He knew in advance that in Rawdon Scudamore he had a part in which he could force recognition of his technical skill and exceptional talent as he could have done at any time in the previous year or so given an opportunity. In any case, although he had still to wait four years before his performance in *The Bells* would carry him to the head of his profession, his reputation and his livelihood were from this time no longer in doubt, and among the distinguished audience who witnessed

[3] Boucicault, Dionysius Lardner, 1822–90. Actor and dramatist. His plays include *The Corsican Brothers, Louis XI, The Shaughraun* and *The Colleen Bawn*. It is possible that he was the first playwright to receive a royalty. His son Dionsysius (Dot) Boucicault, 1859–1929, was also an actor and dramatist.

[4] In London the title was changed to *Hunted Down*.

his first night in London, there were those who already recognised the full extent of his genius.

During the next four years he played sometimes in London, sometimes on tour, once with Sothern in *Our American Cousin* in Paris, when he saw for the first time the technical accomplishment of the actors at the Comédie Française. In 1868 he was engaged by Alfred Wigan to play at the Queen's Theatre in a company which included a young actress named Ellen Terry. They played the leading parts in a new play by Charles Reade which was a failure, a stop-gap revival of *Still Waters Run Deep*, and in *Katherine and Petruchio*, Garrick's version of *The Taming of the Shrew*. Irving found little to admire in Ellen Terry – at that time between her marriage with G. F. Watts and her life with Edward Godwin – who seemed to him frivolous. She in return found him frightening in his fierce application and earnestness of purpose. On Friday nights, always in a hurry to leave the theatre, she accepted the place he politely offered her in the queue waiting for salaries. Years later, talking to Sir Mortimer Menpes, she was to say: 'How conceited he was in those days. Why, he could hardly speak at that time for conceit. But in later years what a difference.'

In 1870 Irving was playing at the Vaudeville Theatre when he received an invitation to meet James Albery. Albery had written a new play *Two Roses* and he had merely sketched in the chief part of Digby Grant in the hope that Irving would play it and help at rehearsal to develop it. *Two Roses*, Albery's only entirely successful play, was in the comedy style of T. W. Robertson, and the part of Digby Grant (who, believing himself to have inherited a title and fortune, snubs his former friends to find his claim rejected in favour of one of them) was a part which Irving again recognised as completely suitable for him and one in which he could this time demonstrate his talent for light comedy.

The play was enormously successful and Digby Grant entered the repertory of classical Victorian parts. The first run of the piece was memorable for an event which opened the last lap of Irving's long journey to eminence. On the two hundred and ninety-first night of the run of the piece he took his benefit and, at the close of the comedy, appearing in evening dress, he announced that he would recite Hood's poem *The Dream of*

Eugene Aram. Then for the first time, without scenery or
properties, he revealed to a London audience the intensity, the
almost hypnotic magnetism and the power to convey terror
and guilt which in a few years' time would make him the
greatest drawing power in the theatre of his day.

In the audience witnessing the performance and the ovation
sat Hezekiah Bateman, an American theatre manager, who,
having at different times had three daughters on the stage, had
now taken a lease of the Lyceum Theatre, where he proposed
to launch his fourth daughter, Isabel. He immediately offered
Irving an engagement at the Lyceum in the following autumn.

Bateman, like so many managers before him, failed at first
to make any use of Irving. His ambitions were centred on his
daughter and, having engaged Irving because he had witnessed
his great powers as a tragedian, he cast him in support of Isabel
Bateman, first as a lovesick peasant in an adaptation from the
French and secondly as Alfred Jingle in a version by Albery of
The Pickwick Papers. When both these plays failed – in spite
of Irving's success as Alfred Jingle – Irving reminded Bateman
of his promise to put on a play called *The Bells*, an adaptation
from a French play, *Le Juif Polonais*, by Erckmann and
Chatrian.

The Bells is part of the history of the theatre. It is not of a
quality to remain in the repertory of acted plays but it aroused
a fervour of enthusiasm in its time which ensured it a place in
the annals of dramatic events. For the rest of Irving's life it
would be so often performed that it is hardly possible to recall
his name without recalling *The Bells*. Writing of later performances Gordon Craig says: 'At his entrance the applause
was so instantaneous that it became part of the play. . . . In *The
Bells*, the hurricane of applause at Irving's entrance was no
interruption . . . it was something that can only be described as
part and parcel of the whole, as right as rain. It was a torrent
while it lasted. Power responded to power.'

The story of the play is of a respected burgomaster who
fifteen years before, the poverty-stricken and despairing father
of a starving family, had on a foul night given shelter to a
Polish Jew and, on a sudden impulse after his guest's departure,
had taken a short cut to a point on his route and there murdered
him for the money he carried. Now, unsuspected and respected,

Sir Squire and
Lady Bancroft

1   Marie Wilton (Bancroft) as
Pippo in *The Maid and the Magpie*,
the burlesque by J. J. Byron in
which Charles Dickens so much
admired her. Strand Theatre, 1858.

2   Marie Bancroft as Polly Eccles
and John Hare as Sam Gerridge
in *Caste* by T. W. Robertson, the
play in which the use of real
china inspired the term 'cup-and-
saucer comedy'. Prince of Wales's
Theatre, 1867.

3 Squire Bancroft in the early nineties.

4 *Diplomacy*. John Hare's production at the Garrick Theatre in 1893 when the Bancrofts returned to the stage to play in it. From left to right: standing, Arthur Cecil, Lady Monckton, Sir Squire Bancroft, John Hare, Johnston Forbes-Robertson. Sitting: Olga Nethersole, Gilbert Hare, Lady Bancroft, Kate Rorke.

5   Irving as Matthias in *The Bells*, Act 2. Counting out the money for his daughter's dowry, Matthias recognises one of the coins that had belonged to the Polish Jew. Lyceum Theatre, 1871.

6   Cartoon of Irving by Max Beerbohm in the possession of the Garrick Club.

7 Irving as the Vicar and Ellen Terry as Olivia in the Lyceum production of *Olivia*, 1885. Between 1880 and 1890 Irving refused to allow any photographs to be taken of himself other than portrait photographs and a few with Ellen Terry in *Olivia*. This is the only one of the two together and is described as 'the only authorized photograph' of Irving as the Vicar and Ellen Terry as Olivia.

8 Ellen Terry in the costume designed by E. W. Godwin for *The Cup* by Alfred Tennyson. Lyceum Theatre, 1881.

Sir Johnston Forbes-Robertson

10, 11, 12 Three Hamlets. *below* At the Lyceum in 1897, *opposite top* his last at his farewell production at Drury Lane in 1913; he wore a similar costume for both productions. *opposite bottom* The film made from this production by Cecil Hepworth, also in 1913. The castle for the ghost scene was built at Lulworth Cove at a cost, then considered very high, of £400.

13 *Caesar and Cleopatra.*
Forbes-Robertson as Caesar, the
role originally written for him by
Bernard Shaw, with his wife
Gertrude Elliot in the first London
production at the Savoy Theatre
in 1907.

14 *The Passing of the Third Floor
Back*, by Jerome K. Jerome. Left
to right: Agnes Thomas as
Mrs Sharpe, Forbes-Robertson as
the Third Floor Back and Gertrude
Elliot as Stasia. St James's Theatre,
1908.

the burgomaster is inwardly haunted by the sound of the bells on his victim's sledge. In the last act of the play, virtually a monologue, the burgomaster dreams of a trial and dies from self-induced terror – a scene which was perfectly conceived for this actor in whom intensity and guilt seemed natural characteristics.

As an actor-producer Irving was pre-eminent and with *The Bells* he for the first time rehearsed the production so that every-thing contributed to his own performance. His contemporaries speak again and again of his almost mesmeric powers and thus raise again and again the question whether he was a great actor or merely a great personality. It is a matter of considerable interest, therefore, that on its first night *The Bells* was followed by *Pickwick*, and Irving showed his versatility by playing Matthias and Alfred Jingle on the same evening.

Irving owed Bateman his opportunity to impress his genius on a London audience. He owed to him, too, his first meeting with William Gorman Wills. Wills was an Irishman, a poet and painter, who was introduced to Bateman by Herman Vezin[5] for whom he had written two plays, neither of them very successful. Bateman, nevertheless, took to Wills and commis-sioned him to write an adaptation of *Medea* for his eldest daughter, Kate, and at his supper table his two protégés met. There began then a partnership which caused Shaw later to describe Wills as the resident playwright at the Lyceum. During the run of *The Bells* Wills prepared a play entitled *Charles I*, a romantic domestic tragedy which owed little to history and much to Irving's noble appearance and his portrayal of the scene in which the King is betrayed by the Earl of Moray and that in which he says farewell to his Queen – played by Isabel Bateman – and his children. Following this Wills made a play of the poem *Eugene Aram*, with which Irving had first startled London. In both these plays Irving increased his hold on the public, and in *Eugene Aram* he bowled out Clement Scott who ended a rapturous notice with the words: 'The task of the play is herculean for any actor; and once more Mr Irving has triumphed.'

Then in *Richelieu*, which Lytton wrote for Macready, Irving

[5] Vezin, Herman, 1829–1910. English actor born in USA but came to England 1850. Played Macbeth, Othello and Iago. Acted with both Irving and Tree.

C

began his challenge to the old masters of his art, on this occasion
not entirely successfully, as for the first time the critics were
divided in their opinions. Over the years, however, *Richelieu*
came to be regarded as one of his greatest parts. In 1879 Jules
Claretie – a future administrator of the Comédie Française,
with whose company Henry James believed nothing in London
could be compared – wrote of him: '*Richelieu* was the first
play in which I saw Mr Irving in London. Here he is superb.
His performance amounts to a resurrection. . . . And what an
artist the tragedian is.'

After *Richelieu* he played Hamlet. It had almost invariably
been the case that, when a great new actor has appeared to
entrapture theatregoers, much of the excitement and astonishment has been because of the *naturalness* of his acting. Whether
it was little Garrick who came 'bounding on to the stage', or
Macklin who inspired Pope to the couplet 'This is the Jew that
Shakespeare drew', or Kean wearing a plain black wig and
making his first appearance as Shylock, they all captured their
audiences by a convincing representation of the character they
played. As the influence of the great actor died, the less talented
body of the profession returned to conventional declamation
and gesticulation, interpretations of an essentially dramatic
kind. This on the whole is easier and is an art that can be
learned, and although there have been very good actors who
cultivated a beautiful voice and practised a formal declamatory
style – as for instance, the Kembles – they have always had to
give way to the genius of an actor who could convince an
audience that he *was* the character he played.[6]

Irving stood against the 'new school', represented by Shaw
and Ibsen and developed at the Court Theatre by Granville
Barker, and today he is thought of as a romantic actor of the
old school; but when he first played Hamlet he departed from
tradition and risked disaster by playing him as a human being.
Laurence Irving says:

Irving's unusual appearance gave the audience their first shock
of bewilderment. Gone were Hamlet's funereal plumes and trap-
pings of woe and the air of pompous melancholy. Irving was,
indeed, dressed in black, relieved only by the gold chain which he

---

[6] Henry James was much influenced by Fanny Kemble, in whose company he used to
visit the theatre, but according to Laurence Irving when acting she spoke of 'Ham-a-lette'.

wore round his neck, and the cold sparkle of his silver sword hilt and sword belt. But his loose fitting tunic, deeply skirted and heavily collared with beaver, was such as a young man of action might have ordered to his own design. . . . His bearing and manner were those of a young aristocrat in whom grace and self-assurance were modestly combined. There was nothing to distract the attention from the pale face framed in his own raven curls; there was little in the expression of his features to deflect the message of the troubled eyes in whose gaze there lurked the hint of sorrow, dejection and suspicion.

For the whole of the first act the success of Irving's Hamlet hung in the balance. Clement Scott writing the next day said:

So subtle is the actor's art, so intense is his application, and so daring his disregard of conventionality, that the first act ends with comparative disappointment. Those who have seen other Hamlets are aghast. Mr. Irving is missing his points, he is neglecting his opportunities . . . but over all, disputants or enthusiasts, has already been thrown an indescribable spell. None can explain it; but all are now spellbound. The Hamlet is 'thinking aloud', as Hazlitt wished. He is as much of the gentleman and scholar as possible and 'as little of the actor'.

Hamlet ran for two hundred nights at the Lyceum – a run equalled by the Bancrofts with modern comedies but never before achieved with Shakespeare. Irving's position at the head of his profession was from now on undisputed.

Hamlet was produced at the Lyceum in October 1874. Four months later Bateman died and Mrs Bateman took over the management. During the next two years under her management Irving appeared as Macbeth and later as Othello. Neither of these parts did much for his reputation, although the production of *Macbeth* ran for eighty nights and that of *Othello* for forty-nine – at that time a record. In both parts Irving gave an unconventional interpretation – playing Macbeth as a craven who shrinks from the crimes to which his murderous ambition has driven him, and Othello with a bronze complexion and in the clothes and armour, designed by Sir John Tenniel, of a serving Venetian general instead of with the dark complexion and in the turbans of tradition. In both parts Irving's powers at this time were inadequate to his conception and: 'For nature,' one critic wrote, 'we got exaggeration; for elocution, scolding; for affection, melancholy; and for deportment, tricks.' In spite of which, Henry James, who could never reconcile himself to the idea that Irving was a great tragic actor and who wrote of his performance of Macbeth in the same tone of baffled disbelief he invariably used when speaking of him, had on this occasion one or two good things to say.

He has been much criticized for his conception of his part – for making Macbeth so spiritless a plotter before his crime, and so arrant a coward afterward. But in the text, as he seeks to emphasize it, there is fair warrant for the line he follows. Mr. Irving has great skill in the representation of terror, and it is quite open to him to have thrown into relief this side of the part. His best moment is his rendering of the scene with the bloody daggers – though it must be confessed that this stupendous scene always does much toward acting itself. Mr. Irving, however, is here altogether admirable, and his representation of a nature trembling and quaking to its innermost spiritual recesses really excites the imagination. Only a trifle less powerful is his scene with Banquo's ghost at the feast, and the movement with which, exhausted with vain bravado, he muffles his head in his mantle and collapses beside the throne.

The season of 1876, although it ended with a successful revival of *Hamlet*, marked a decline in the fortunes of the Lyceum and of Henry Irving. All his life Irving took successful productions on tour in the provinces and thereby built up a nation-wide audience who would restore his fortunes and his confidence when London was adverse. In the autumn of this year he took out the production of *Hamlet, Charles I* and *The Bells*. 'My success,' he wrote to a friend, 'has been far beyond my expectation – surprising. But *Hamlet* is *the* thing and swamps all else – which makes my work very hard.' Of the seventy-eight performances which the tour entailed, fifty-six were of *Hamlet*.

This tour was important not merely for its phenomenal success but because in Dublin Irving met Bram Stoker. Stoker was a civil servant who also wrote dramatic criticism for the *Dublin Mail*. He impressed Irving originally by the understanding he showed in his articles and indelibly by bursting into hysterics after a private recital of *Eugene Aram*. Bram Stoker became Irving's business and acting manager, served him all his life and after his death wrote his biography. During this tour Irving also engaged H. J. Loveday as stage manager for the Lyceum. Loveday's father had been musical director at Drury Lane when Edmund Kean was acting there, and both he and his wife are described by Laurence Irving as 'trusted and perceptive witnesses' who could describe to Irving Kean's performances 'with every nuance of gesture and inflection'. Thus it is possible that in Sir Laurence Olivier's Richard we saw something of Edmund Kean.

Richard III was produced at the Lyceum Theatre on 29 January 1877. Irving, very conscious of the partial failure of *Macbeth* and *Othello*, had given great thought to the production. Since 1700, when Colley Cibber[7] re-wrote Shakespeare's play, all Irving's predecessors from Garrick to Macready had used his version. Irving's *Richard III* is memorable not merely because the part was so admirably suited to his talents but also because for the first time in nearly two hundred years he restored Shakespeare's Richard to the stage.

By the end of the evening Irving had won back his position as the greatest living actor of Shakespeare, and it was now that the esteem in which he was hereafter to be held by the members of his own profession began to be demonstrated. After the performance he was presented with a sword which Edmund Kean had used as Richard and with David Garrick's ring in which was mounted a miniature of Shakespeare.

In 1878 Irving wrote to Mrs Bateman asking her permission to engage a leading lady of his own choice who would give him stronger support than Isabel Bateman was able to do and who would bring with her a personal following. Mrs Bateman, who seems to have been aware that her leading man had over the last few years developed a strength which must finally burst the bonds of their business relationship, replied that she could not for Isabel's sake accept his suggestion but offered to allow him to take the Lyceum Theatre off her hands. By August of that year she announced the transfer of the lease of the Lyceum to Irving and her own intention to move with Isabel to Sadler's Wells. Thus by her generosity she solved easily a situation that would have had to be solved in some way; but

---

[7] Cibber, Colley, 1671–1757. Actor, playwright and theatre manager. Part of the 'Triumvirate' that managed Drury Lane. He re-wrote *Richard III* interpolating scenes from *Henry V* and *Henry VI: Part III*, freely embellishing the text.

Irving felt always a little uneasy towards the Batemans until late in life Isabel wrote to him expressly forgiving him for anything there might have been to forgive.

Before opening at the Lyceum as manager he was committed to a provincial tour. He paid one visit to the theatre before he left London to see Ellen Terry at the Court. Then he invited her to become his leading lady when he returned.

In 1863, while playing in Manchester, Irving, still a poor and unknown provincial actor, had met and fallen in love with a young actress named Nellie Moore. Nellie Moore, who is described as having a round and intelligent face, wide-set eyes, a fair complexion and a mass of golden hair, was very talented and already successful, and had come to play in Manchester between two London engagements. Too poor and as yet occupying too humble a position in her own profession to think of proposing marriage to her, Irving nevertheless became her constant companion while she remained in Manchester and wrote to her constantly when she returned to London. Then in 1866, when he achieved success in London in the part of Rawdon Scudamore, he resumed his relationship with her on more equal terms.

At this time in his life Irving began, because of his great success, to be asked about in London society. One evening he was on his way to a party given by Clement Scott, the dramatic critic of the *Daily Telegraph*, when there occurred one of those strange long shots, which, more credible in the smaller society of that day, make one wonder whether the coincidences of Victorian novels are really so improbable as they seem. When Irving arrived at what he believed to be his destination, he entered the wrong house. As the maid was explaining to him his error the daughter of the house, Miss Florence O'Callaghan, came into the hall bound, like himself, for Clement Scott's party. Miss O'Callaghan was an ardent play-goer; she immediately recognised Irving and during the evening became infatuated with him. From now on she made it her business to keep in touch with him, although he, still in love with Nellie Moore, was not seriously responsive.

There came a time, however, when his relationship with Nellie Moore was, for reasons that are not known, broken.

Laurence Irving suggests that some imagined slight may have come between them but it seems possible that, in spite of the fact that they loved each other, the difference between them was not imagined but inevitable to two proud and sensitive natures, ambitious in the same profession. In any case, whatever the reason of their parting, the fact of it was soon known to Miss O'Callaghan, who now made more open and more successful advances to Irving. He, no doubt sore at losing Nellie Moore, was in a mood to respond and the fact that her parents were initially against the attachment seems only to have strengthened it. From the beginning, however, the characters and the lives of these young people made them unsuited to each other. During Irving's engagement with Alfred Wigan at the Queen's Theatre, Nellie Moore joined the company, provoking a letter from Florence to Irving expressing anxiety at this renewed association and criticism of the actress. Irving's reply is notable both as an example of the strength and nobility which are often attributed to him and for the asperity with which he treated a rather natural jealousy.

I received both letters today. Although somewhat prepared for the contents of the first, I was, perhaps, a little astonished. It is painful to murmur any fault of those whom we regard and to conceal the wherefore. Say of her to me, Flo, what you will – I willingly accept it, but sayings or opinions of others keep back – especially expressions of condescension. These I cannot endure. They tingle through my veins and cause my blood to circulate at a rate to a phlegmatic man – objectionable.
The end all is that our position is as before. I will do all I can to trust in you. . . .

Then in 1869 Nellie Moore died. While leaving the house in which she died Irving was met by a friend, Miss Friswell, who attempted to sympathise with him. He replied: 'It is not always a misfortune to die young.' Laurence Irving writes:

His remark was not a careless one; death, he suspected, had spared Nellie Moore much unhappiness. Before she died he had discovered that a supposed friend had come between them and, although he had no conclusive evidence, he had good cause to believe she had suffered grave injury at his hands.
Later, in cold anger, he confronted this man and made it clear to him that although evidence of his guilt had been buried with his

victim, suspicion would rest upon him as long as his accuser lived. Toole, fearful for Irving's self-control, was near at hand and never forgot the faces of the two men when they came from the room in which they had faced one another alone. The wound in Brodribb's heart never healed; the armour of Irving was tempered further by this cold shock of personal tragedy.

This is a curious passage, written in terms so like those of Irving's own melodramas that one cannot help suspecting that it was inspired by the account of some 'henchman'. It seems beyond doubt that we are meant to understand from 'a grave injury . . . buried with her' that Nellie Moore died of a pregnancy, or, since death from an early pregnancy is unusual, from an abortion, but, as even the name of this actress is now unknown to us except in this connection, there seems no reason not to say so. In the same way there is a lack of conviction in this talk of 'cold anger' and 'cold shock', which is of a piece with the further information that when Irving died a photograph of Nellie Moore was found in his pocket book pasted to the back of one of himself.

Irving was undoubtedly a normal heterosexual male and, although the facts are wrapped in mystery, there seem to have been only short periods of his life when he had no attachment to any woman. Nevertheless, he was a man with a vocation and only one true love – the stage. Shaw said that 'Irving would not have left the stage for a night to spend it with Helen of Troy' and Gordon Craig wrote : 'So devoted was Irving to our stage, that he really was innocently selfish. My mother often used to say, with a lovely twinkle in her eyes, "Yes, yes – were I to be run over by a steamroller tomorrow, Henry would be deeply grieved : would say quietly 'What a pity!' and would add, after two moments' reflection : 'Who is there – er – to go on for her tonight?' " '

Men whose lives are dedicated to their profession often find a woman who is prepared to devote herself entirely to them. Irving failed to find anyone of this kind until possibly when late in life he met Mrs Aria. Before that he was driven to leave the women who loved him, including his mother, in circumstances connected with his profession. He lived in a romantic age and had an unusually romantic temperament. It is not surprising that it pleased him to believe that the love of his life died young – even though she died separated from him and pregnant by another man – but it is curious that the notion should be so unquestionably accepted by other people.

When Florence O'Callaghan's parents withdrew their opposition, she and Irving were married. From the first there seemed little chance of happiness. Florence was vain, bad-tempered, snobbish and unloving. A few days before their marriage Irving wrote to her:

I hope my dearest with all my soul that when the day is past an end will be put to all reproaches from you or misunderstandings by me.

On Sunday night your manner I thought was unsurmountably cold. It was but thought I hope. Nothing I think could so soon dull affection in man or woman as indifference.

You at first lavished on me such love that if I became spoiled – the fault is all your own. But you still love me as you did – don't you my darling? *Answer this.*

Irving was married to Florence O'Callaghan in July 1869. By 1870 she was pregnant and he studying the part of Digby Grant in *Two Roses*. All his life he enjoyed the company of actors and one of the pleasures he had hoped for in a home of his own was to bring them back to supper after the evening's work. His wife could already not disguise her dislike of his friends and of these supper parties, and thus early in his married life the atmosphere of nagging disapproval in his home drove him to hire a cheap lodging in which to study his part in peace. Irving was an affectionate and proud father and the birth of his first child brought the couple together again. But not for long. It is not too much to say that Florence seems almost to have hated him. When he was at home she nagged him, when he was on tour she wrote reproving him for spending money on a reasonably comfortable room. Later in 1870 they parted but early in the following year Florence came to Irving and begged him to return to her. He at once agreed to her request and soon after wrote to her: 'At once disabuse your mind, dear, of any desire of mine to delay our union. I am more than anxious to be with you and our child.'

After their reunion Florence conceived their second child and Irving joined Bateman at the Lyceum. In the autumn of the following year he appeared in *The Bells*.

When Kean made his first success in *The Merchant of Venice* he spoke to no one at the theatre but went straight home to his wife. 'Mary,' he is supposed to have said to her, 'Charles shall go to Eton and you shall ride in your carriage and pair.' After the enormous success of *The Bells* and following a supper party at which Irving received the ecstatic praise and congratulations of everyone around him – a scene of excitement and jubilation from which his wife held curiously aloof – he drove home with her in a brougham. As they were crossing Hyde Park Corner he laid his hand on her arm and said: 'Well my dear, we too shall soon have our carriage and pair.' This innocent and modest reference to his own success was too much for his wife's jealous hostility. 'Are you going on making a fool of yourself like this all your life?' she asked.

Irving stopped the driver of the brougham, got down and, in one of the most dramatic partings in history, walked away. He never returned to his wife and he never spoke to her again. He left with her his two sons, one as yet unborn.

Ellen Terry, like Marie Wilton and Madge Robertson, was born to a theatre family and her parents, like the Robertsons, could find a juvenile stock company from among their offspring. Ellen made her first appearance at the age of nine in Charles Kean's company, playing the child Mamillius in *The Winter's Tale*. From this time onwards she lived the hard life of the professional actor, rehearsing by day and playing by night, dropping to sleep in the Green Room when she was released from the stage. She was taught her professional technique by Mrs Kean, of whom she later wrote: 'No one ever had a sharper tongue or a kinder heart than Mrs Kean. Beginning with her I have always loved women with a somewhat hard manner. I have never believed in their hardness, and have proved them tender and generous to the extreme.'

Mrs Kean's heart may have been particularly soft towards this graceful child, who could walk naturally with a blanket pinned round her waist and trailing several inches on the ground. The critic Dutton Cook said of Kate and Ellen Terry that their talents went far beyond the usual charm of well-trained child players. 'A peculiar dramatic sensitiveness and susceptibility characterized the sisters Terry; their nervous organization, their mental impressibility and vivaciousness not less than their personal charms and attractions, may be said to have ordained and determined their success upon the stage.'

In 1862, when Ellen Terry was fifteen, these two impressionable and talented girls were sent to visit the painter, G. F. Watts, Kate to sit for him and Ellen to chaperone her while she did so. Watts was weak, indolent, idealistic, melancholic and hypochondriacal and he was dominated all his life by a series of patronesses. Yet in addition to his artistic talents he must have had immense charm because, until very late in his life when he married a woman much younger than himself, he was passed from the family of one woman prepared to devote herself to his interests to that of another. At this time he was living at Little Holland House in London with Mr and Mrs Thoby Prinsep.

The two girls were sent to him by the playwright, Tom Taylor, because Watts had seen Kate on the stage and had wished to paint her. At Little Holland House Ellen saw spacious rooms and beautiful things for the first time in her life, and she fell in love with it, with Watts's paintings and a little with Watts himself. Watts at this time had the idea that he needed a wife and he believed himself in love with Ellen. One day he kissed her. Years later she wrote to Shaw: 'I told no one for a fortnight, but when I was alone with Mother one day she looked so pretty and sad and kind, I told her – what do you think I told the poor darling? I told her I *must* be married to him *now* because I was going to have a baby!!!! *and she* believed me. Oh, I tell you I thought I knew everything then, but I was nearly 16 years old then – and I was *sure* that kiss meant giving me a baby.'

Mrs Prinsep was prepared to do anything to meet the artistic needs of the 'Signor', as Watts was known to this household and she is believed to have thought that, if Watts wished to marry, this unformed young girl would make a suitably malleable wife. So before Ellen was seventeen, she left the stage to marry Watts, who was then forty-seven.

Ellen Terry spent much of her married life in Watts's studio, where she posed continuously. He afterwards destroyed many of the sketches he made of her but among the portraits that can be seen today in public galleries are 'Ellen Terry' in the

National Portrait Gallery and 'Ophelia' in the Watts Gallery, while 'Choosing' and 'The Sisters' are in private collections. This was generally a very productive period of Watts's life and if, as is seldom questioned, this was the only consummation of the marriage, it is also true that her association with Watts permanently benefited Ellen Terry. Graham Robertson says of her: 'Her charm held everyone, but I think pre-eminently those who loved pictures. She was *par excellence* the Painter's Actress and appealed to the eye before the ear; her gesture and pose were eloquence itself.' Mrs Prinsep, however, was not well satisfied. She found the high-spirited and talented girl infinitely less manageable than she had hoped and she persuaded Watts that his young wife was a disruptive influence in his life. Then Ellen committed an indiscretion which gave Mrs Prinsep her opportunity, and to her indignation and shame she was sent home to her parents. Five weeks later a deed of separation was signed in which the cause of separation was set down as 'incompatibility of temper' and Watts agreed to pay his wife £300 a year 'so long as she shall lead a chaste life'.

Ellen was completely bewildered and very unhappy. During her married life she had had, she later asserted, 'not one single pang of regret for the theatre'. 'I wondered at the new life and worshipped it because of its beauty,' she said, while the marriage, 'was in many ways very happy indeed'. I was miserable, indignant, unable to understand that there could be any justice in what had happened.'

Ellen did not need to work because she had £6 a week from Watts, but after a while she was 'practically *driven*' back to the stage by her parents and by Tom Taylor. It was during this period that she appeared in *Katherine and Petruchio*, Garrick's shortened version of *The Taming of the Shrew*, opposite a serious young actor called Henry Irving.

Then in the spring of 1868 she left the stage for the second time without word or warning to her family, and disappeared into the country to set up house with the architect E. W. Godwin. Ellen Terry had two children by Godwin who later became known to the world as Edith Craig and Edward Gordon Craig. She lived with him for six years at Harpenden and she loved him very much. At first their love was a great happiness to both but they were short of money and Godwin had to work in London. There was no telephone and, as time went on and he became busy, he had no means of letting her know whether or not he was coming home. There are sad tales of Ellen's harnessing the pony and driving to the station at night, only to drive home again alone; and others, almost equally sad, of how when he did come he discovered that his talented, beautiful but unpractical love had failed to provide any food for his supper. Above all, they had too little money and in the end the bailiffs tramped up the garden path. Then there occurred the famous meeting with Charles Reade.

Charles Reade, the novelist, was also the author of a number of plays, among the most famous of which were *The Courier of Lyons*, revived by Irving as *The Lyons Mail*, *It's Never Too Late to Mend* and, in collaboration with Tom Taylor, the Peg Woffington play, *Masks and Faces*. Both he and Tom Taylor were devoted to the Terry sisters, whom they had known as children, Tom Taylor's favourite being perhaps Kate, while Charles Reade adored Ellen.

In the winter of 1873–4 Charles Reade, in full pink, went out hunting in the Harpenden area. Jumping a hedge into a lane, he came across a young woman struggling with a pony trap, the wheel of which had come off. He went up to her to offer assistance and recognised Ellen Terry.

'Good God,' he cried, 'it's Nelly. Where have you been all these years?'

When she said she had been having a very happy time, he replied: 'Well, you've had it long enough,' and commanded her to come back to the stage in a play called *The Wandering Heir* which he was about to put on. Ellen, remembering the children and the bailiffs, replied that she would do so for £40 a week, and, in the words of Roger Manvell, 'England's greatest actress since Sarah Siddons returned to the stage, very unwillingly, and through a chance meeting with an old friend in a country lane'.

Charles Reade, who was responsible for teaching her a great deal at this time, has left a famous description of her. 'Ellen Terry is an enigma. Her eyes are pale, her nose rather long, her mouth nothing particular. Complexion a delicate brick-dust, her hair rather like tow. Yet somehow she is *beautiful*. Her expression *kills* any pretty face you see beside her. Her figure is lean and boney; her hand masculine in size and form. Yet she is a pattern of fawn-like grace. Whether in movement or repose, grace pervades the hussy.' He also said of her: 'A young lady highly gifted with what Voltaire calls *le grand art de plaire*.'

When Ellen Terry first came back to London Godwin took and furnished for her a house in Taviton Street. Godwin was interested in theatre design and had lately written a series of articles entitled 'The Architecture and Costume of Shakespeare's Plays'. At Taviton Street he covered the floor of the drawing room with straw-coloured matting and hung cretonne with a Japanese pattern in delicate grey-blue on the white walls. The furniture was of wickerwork and in the centre of the room he placed a full-sized caste of the Venus de Milo. Presently, however, the bailiffs appeared again, so that on the historic occasion when Mrs Bancroft called on Ellen Terry, apart from the young actress herself, she found nothing in the room but the Venus de Milo. Looking at this, she put her hand to her eyes in her best farcical manner and murmured 'Dear me!' Then she asked Ellen Terry if she would come to the Prince of Wales's Theatre to play Portia in *The Merchant of Venice*. She added that Mr Godwin would be asked to take over the archaeological supervision of the production design.

In spite of the failure of *The Merchant of Venice*, Squire Bancroft claimed that Ellen Terry's performance was the foundation stone of her brilliant career. Writing about it herself, she said:

I had had some success in other parts, and had tasted the delights of knowing that audiences liked me, and had liked them back again. But never until I appeared as Portia at the Prince of Wales's had I experienced that awe-struck feeling which comes, I suppose, to no actress more than once in a lifetime – the feeling of the conqueror. In homely parlance I knew that I had 'got them' at the moment when I spoke the speech beginning, 'You see me, Lord Bassanio, where I stand.'

After this she appeared for the Bancrofts in Lytton's comedy *Money*, and, for one night only, as Pauline in *The Lady of Lyons;* she played a supporting role to Mrs Bancroft in Reade and Taylor's *Masks and Faces*, and finally Blanche Haye in Robertson's comedy *Ours*. It is said that by now her success was not altogether to the taste of Mrs Bancroft, and indeed it would have been very remarkable if it had been. In the autumn of the year 1876, she went to the Court Theatre under the management of John Hare.

He commissioned W. G. Wills (Irving's resident playwright) to adapt *The Vicar of Wakefield* for the stage and, re-named *Olivia*, this play became a valuable property for Ellen Terry for almost as long as she remained on the stage. At the time of its first performance it caused a fashion, Olivia hats and kerchiefs and Ellen Terry photographs being on sale everywhere.

By now Godwin had left her and in January 1876 he married his student, Beatrice Phillips. Gordon Craig writing of his parents' separation said: 'Then by mutual disagreement they parted. Sad: but there was no unkindness, no dissension – they were neither of them desertable people.' By this he meant that his mother was not a desertable person. Godwin left her and she never made any secret of her love for him or of her unhappiness when their relationship, which had been frayed by poverty, came to an end.

In March 1877 Watts instituted proceedings for divorce and in November of that year Ellen Terry married Charles Wardell, who acted in the company at the Court Theatre in the name of Charles Kelly. Edy, Ellen Terry's daughter, was to say of her: 'All through her life the man of brains competed for her affections with the man of brawn.' Wardell was rather the man of brawn and Ellen Terry appears to have married him mainly to give her children a name. The strange conventions of the society of her time were satisfied by this gesture and her parents, from whom she had been separated since her elopement with Godwin, were gladly reconciled to her and to their two small grandchildren. These now became overnight Edith and Edward Wardell. The Wardell family moved into 33 Longridge Road, Earls Court and it was here that Henry Irving called on Ellen Terry to invite her to become his leading lady.

The partnership between Henry Irving and Ellen Terry lasted for twenty years and was the most memorable in the history of the theatre. Henry Irving's qualities as an actor have already been discussed. Ellen Terry's consisted primarily in a radiance of personality and all-conquering charm, but she had also a

mastery of technique which enabled her to deploy a very considerable talent. Apart from her extraordinary power to please,
the quality for which she was most famous was her naturalness.
Graham Robertson, an ardent playgoer who knew her well, has
left these memories of her most famous roles.

As Portia I think she must have realised almost everyone's
ideal – she *was* Portia; as Beatrice she realised something so far
above *my* ideal that I could hardly recognise the character, for I
have the bad taste not to admire Beatrice.

For the (in my eyes) noisy, pushing, unmannerly, Messinine minx
Ellen Terry contrived to substitute a wholly delightful creature
whose bubbling and infectious high spirits were never allowed to
hide her gentle kindliness and well-bred grace of manner.

From what she evolved her I have never made out; I cannot find
her in the play, even with the aid of the crib supplied by Miss Terry,
but I hope that my blindness is at fault and that Shakespeare really
wrote the part as she played it.

Her Cordelia, he says, captured all hearts; 'Lovely and gracious,
she was Cordelia as she had been Portia, though I regret to say
that, when studying the character, she wrote "FOOL" in large
letters against the young lady's refusal to admit her love for
her old father.' It was as Imogen, the last great Shakespearean
part she played at the Lyceum, that she outdid all former
achievements. 'Her scene of joy, on receiving the false letter, a
joy so great that sorrow must needs be close behind, was
absolutely overwhelming; it moved to tears.'

Ellen Terry never played Rosalind because there is no part
in *As You Like It* which suited Henry Irving, but this was so
much lamented and the felicities she might have brought to
the role so often imagined that the absence of her Rosalind
made almost as much mark on the annals of the play as the
greatest performances of it.

Throughout Henry Irving's life there would always be those
who could not appreciate the qualities which won from others
so much ardent admiration. Ellen Terry pleased everyone save
Henry James. He complained that she lacked the polish and
finish of the actresses of the Comédie Française and he could
not find compensation in the qualities peculiarly her own. He
wrote:

By many intelligent persons she is regarded as an actress of exquisite genius, and is supposed to impart an extraordinary interest to everything that she touches. This is not, in our opinion, the truth, and yet to gainsay the assertion too broadly is to fall into an extreme of injustice. The difficulty is that Miss Terry has charm – remarkable charm; and this beguiles people into thinking her an accomplished actress. There is a natural quality about her that is extremely pleasing – something wholesome and English and womanly which often touches easily where art, to touch, has to be finer than we often see it.

Yet a great deal of technique – in Ellen Terry's case learned from the time when as a child she played for Mrs Charles Kean – goes into an appearance of naturalness on the stage. Ellen Terry invariably gave a lively intelligence and a great deal of hard work to the parts she played and people who saw her annotated texts or with whom she discussed the professional aspects of her life were often amazed.

It is true, however, that the quality which made her the idol of London in her youth and a legend in her old age and which, in her written words, is still compelling, was charm. Her charm consisted in a splendid generosity of spirit and a great joy in life as well as physical and mental attributes which defy analysis. One of her physical attractions was her voice, about which Bernard Shaw said: 'Her slightly veiled voice reached the remotest listener in the theatre without apparent effort, though the nervous athleticism behind it was of championship quality.' And Henry James, having said that her countenance was happily adapted to the expression of pathetic emotion, went on: 'To this last effect her voice also contributes: it has a sort of monotonous husky thickness which is extremely touching, although it gravely interferes with the modulation of many of her speeches.'

Tributes to Ellen Terry abound in the memoirs of the day but George Bernard Shaw, who loved her, wrote of her unforgettably. He said 'Ellen Terry is the most beautiful name in the world; it rings like a chime through the last quarter of the nineteenth century.' And: 'Every famous man of the last quarter of the nineteenth century, providing he were a theatre-goer, had been in love with Ellen Terry.' And in a comparison with Irving:

They both had beautiful and interesting faces, but faces like Irving's have looked at the world for hundreds of years past from portraits of churchmen, statesmen, princes and saints, while Ellen Terry's face had never been seen in the world before. The much-abused word 'unique' is literally true of Ellen Terry. If Shakespeare had met Irving in the street, he would have recognised a distinguished but familiar type. Had he met Ellen Terry, he would have stared at a new and irresistibly attractive species of womankind.

And, speaking of a chance meeting with her when she was growing old, he wrote:

She was astonishingly beautiful. She had passed through that middle phase, so trying to handsome women, of matronly amplitude, and was again tall and slender, with a new delicacy and intensity in her saddened expression. . . . She asked me why I did not give her some work in the theatre. 'I do not expect leading parts,' she said: 'I am too old. I am quite willing to play a charwoman. I should like to play a charwoman.' 'What would become of the play?' I said. 'Imagine a play in which the part of a canal barge was played by a battleship! What would happen to my play, or to anyone else's, if whenever the charwoman appeared the audience forgot the hero and heroine, and could think of nothing but the wonderful things that charwoman was going to say and do?' It was unanswerable; and we both, I think, felt rather inclined to cry.

But when Ellen Terry joined Irving at the Lyceum she was not old. She was thirty-one.

The productions at the Lyceum were an advance on anything previously seen in the theatre and were notable for their taste and quality and for a lavish expenditure of money, time and trouble. Hawes Craven, who was in charge of the scene-painting, was a master craftsman and the design of the sets was often undertaken by the famous artists of the day. Edward Burne-Jones designed the sets for Tennyson's *King Arthur* and Alma-Tadema those for *Henry VIII, Coriolanus* and *Cymbeline;* while Edward Godwin, at Ellen Terry's request, advised on the scenes and dresses for *The Cup*, also by Tennyson, and Sir Arthur Sullivan was responsible for the incidental music of the productions of *Olivia, Macbeth* and *King Arthur*.

Irving was a great stage-manager and we are told that he

personally superintended every detail of the productions – setting, lighting, even music. William Archer said of him: 'Mr Irving has the art of inspiring to the verge of genius his scenic artists and machinists.... There rises to the mind a whole gallery of scenic pictures, each as worthy of minute study as any canvas of the most learned archaeological painter.' And Ellen Terry tells of the effort that went to the achievement of these results: 'When there was a question of his playing Napoleon his room in Grafton Street was filled with Napoleonic literature. Busts of Napoleon, pictures of Napoleon, relics of Napoleon were everywhere.... It was not Napoleon that interested Henry Irving, but *Napoleon for his purpose* – two very different things.'

It was sometimes suggested that Ellen Terry herself was responsible for the beauty and quality of the Lyceum productions. But her son Gordon Craig denies this. She had, he says, a woman's taste for lovely things and was responsive to music, painting, sculpture and architecture, 'but creative as a stage producer, no'.

She was, nevertheless, influential, and particularly so over the costumes. Many of her own were designed by her friend Alice Comyns Carr and in later days by her daughter, Edy. Materials were often more gorgeous than those of today, but they were less various, and stage effects were sometimes contrived by curious means. The dress worn by Ellen Terry in *Macbeth*, in which Sargent painted her, was made of a yarn crocheted in green silk and blue tinsel which gave the effects of scales; it was sewn all over with real green beetle wings and had a narrow border in Celtic designs worked out in rubies and diamonds. To this was originally added a cloak of velvet in heather tones upon which great griffins were worked in flame-coloured tinsel – but Irving, seeing this cloak at rehearsal, appropriated it for himself.

Irving's method at rehearsal was to begin by reading the whole play aloud to his company, acting every part including his own. From the very start he imposed on the actors his interpretation of their roles, which were in all cases, except that of Ellen Terry, merely in support of his own. Gordon Craig said that at the Lyceum 'an important part was like the leg of a table – not much to look at', and that 'a good actor was one who could do the bit he was given to do and do it as he was told to do it.' Irving was often criticised for surrounding himself with mediocre actors, although most of the famous actors of the day passed at one time or another through the Lyceum school – but his method allowed no place for greatness except in himself. There was an absolute integrity about his egotism. He saw the picture as a whole and in the middle of the picture he saw himself. His loyalty was entirely to the picture and it would have been quite impossible for him to compose it in any way except to enhance and set off the central figure. Therefore he sought good supporting players and he drilled and drilled them until 'the skin grew tight over his face' and 'he became livid with fatigue yet still beautiful', but they became strong and reliable as table legs.

Bernard Shaw complained that the taste and judgment which allowed Irving to achieve so much visual beauty did not extend to literature and, speaking of Irving's performance as King Arthur in the play by J. Comyns Carr, he said: 'While the voice, the gesture, the emotion expressed are those of a hero-king, the talk is the talk of an angry and jealous coster-monger . . .'

Max Beerbohm also had something to say about Irving's taste in literature. In a review of a book called *Impressions of Henry Irving*, he said:

If I had been, like Mr. Pollock, constantly in touch with Irving, and charged thoroughly with his magnetism . . . then perhaps . . . I should, like Mr. Pollock, not dare to breathe on the legend that Irving was, in addition to his genius for acting, a great scholar and a man of exceedingly fine taste in literature. Mr. Pollock must know, none better, how absolute a legend this is; but he will not breathe on it. In 'Much Ado About Nothing' Irving 'fell upon employing an entirely modern phrase' as an 'aside' in one of the dialogues with Beatrice. Some weeks later Mr. Pollock saw the play again, and the offending 'aside' was still in use. Then he spoke to Irving who was grateful for the hint. For 'by an oversight' read 'because he did not know any better.' Left to act for himself, Mr. Pollock was always bold enough to help Irving in matters of litera-ture. But he was, on occasion at any rate, easily deflected by 'a light, meaning touch' on his arm from 'one of the trusted and con-fidential marshals' who guarded Irving's majesty. One evening 'Irving was sympathetically and generously enthusiastic over

Tennyson's work, and, referring to the beautiful lines beginning
"There was a little fair-hair'd Norman maid" – a speech which he
always delivered as one rapt in it – he expressed a strong doubt
if there was anything in Shakespeare to be preferred to it.' Mr.
Pollock, 'startled' – but was he really startled? – 'by such a delivery
from such a source,' was about to protest. when he felt the afore-
said touch on the arm, and said nothing. I wonder if it was Mr.
Loveday, that faithful henchman, who administered the touch.
Irving was trying various sets of sledge-bells for 'The Bells.' He
'began to eliminate them one by one until one set was left for final
consideration. Then he listened more carefully than ever to that set,
and then he turned to Mr. Loveday, a very accomplished musician,
and said: "Now isn't that the right set?" – a question which provoked an emphatic "Not a doubt about it" ' – an answer which
Mr. Pollock offers as a proof of Irving's omniscience, and not having
the slightest element of comedy in it.

The voice of the henchman can also be heard in the following
passage from Laurence Irving on Irving as musician. Having
explained that Sir Arthur Sullivan had written a piece of music
for certain alarums and trumpets, he says:

The result was dismissed by Irving as wholly inappropriate – 'as
music it's very fine – but for our purpose it's no good at all'. Sullivan
asked Irving to try and explain what he had in mind. The actor,
thereupon, with a combination of rhythmic pantomime and suggestive hummings, strove to convey his idea of what was needed.
Sullivan grasped his meaning which he translated rapidly into
musical phrases; when these were rehearsed, he and Irving agreed
that they were musically and dramatically right.

Nevertheless, the zeal of the henchman must not be allowed
to diminish appreciation of Irving's total commitment or the
splendour of many of his productions. Ellen Terry was to write:
'When I am asked what I remember about the first ten years at
the Lyceum, I can answer in one word: Work. I was hardly
ever out of the theatre. What with acting, rehearsing, and
studying – twenty-five reference books were a simple "coming-
in" for one part – I sometimes thought I should go blind and
mad.' And:

The men were as much like him when they tried to carry out his
instructions as brass is like gold; but he never grew weary of
'coaching' them, down to the most minute detail. Once during the

rehearsals of 'Hamlet' I saw him growing more and more fatigued with his efforts to get the actors who opened the play to perceive his meaning. He wanted the first voice to ring out like a pistol shot.

'Who's there?'

'Do give it up,' I said, 'it's no better!'

'Yes, it's a little better,' he answered quietly, 'and so it's worth doing.'

His ruthless conduct of rehearsals often resulted in his being at his worst on first nights. When dead tired in body and mind he assumed his place in the centre of the picture, the weaknesses of his voice and physique often prevented him from doing himself justice. By the third or fourth night his performance was often transformed.

Shakespearean productions at the Lyceum included *Coriolanus, Cymbeline, Hamlet, King Lear, Macbeth, The Merchant of Venice, Much Ado About Nothing, Othello, Richard III, Romeo and Juliet* and *Twelfth Night*. Irving failed as Othello and as King Lear because his voice could not sustain the great moments of these roles and he fell to raving and ranting. He was not much praised as Romeo, although his production was very successful with the public and ran for over 100 nights, partly because he was too old when he played the part and partly because as an actor he never seemed young. But he was as memorable as Shylock, Hamlet and Richard III, and Ellen Terry equally so as Portia, Ophelia, Beatrice and Imogen. Sir John Gielgud, writing in 1963 of the Lyceum production of *Much Ado About Nothing*, said:

An outstandingly successful production of a classical play can kill that play's popularity for many years afterwards. So it happened in Engand with *Much Ado About Nothing*.

Henry Irving produced the play at the Lyceum Theatre in 1882, with himself as Benedick and Ellen Terry as Beatrice, and afterwards revived it several times during his twenty years of management in London, besides touring it in the English provinces and in America. Ellen Terry presented it again under her own management in 1901, with Matheson Lang and later Harcourt Williams, as Benedick. But subsequent revivals, during the succeeding forty years or so were not greatly successful, and playgoers and critics too young to remember Ellen Terry seemed to find the play ill-balanced and even tedious and unconvincing.

As an actor-manager Irving was chiefly criticised because, when not playing Shakespeare, he stuck to the old melodramas or to new plays in the old romantic tradition. Twenty years earlier this criticism might not have occurred to anyone and behind it lay the real charges that he refused to play Ibsen and (largely put forward by Shaw) that he refused to play Shaw.

Irving came at the end of a long tradition of romantic actors and he was never more old-fashioned than his public or than nine out of ten contemporary writers for the stage. He was always looking for new plays and he produced as many as he believed had a reasonable chance of financial success, numbering Tennyson among his dramatists. However, he had a great theatre to fill : the day would come when Ibsen and Shaw could fill a theatre, but it had not come yet. Pioneers acted the plays of both writers for one or two performances at a financial loss. Neither writer could with any certainty have paid the bill for Irving's stage hands alone.

Looking back over almost 100 years we are no longer concerned with the old or new fashion of the Lyceum productions, but with their quality. The truth is that Henry Irving was in the same predicament as almost all theatre managers throughout history. Actors of genius greatly outnumber playwrights of genius, good actors abound, good playwrights are far to seek. The best actors of every generation have been forced to lean heavily on the classics and on rivals of recent successes.

There is no doubt, however, that Irving actually enjoyed fustian and, whereas Ellen Terry was never happy in such parts as Pauline in *The Lady of Lyons*, he delighed in Claud Melnotte. But audiences, too, revelled in this incredible old play and the Lyceum repertory of melodrama and romantic drama drew, not merely the ordinary public, but also the intelligentsia of London. Irving cannot be criticised, as a poet or painter might be, for not being in advance of his time, because it is the nature of the actor's interpretative art that it cannot exist without the active participation of the public. Not for him the uncertain consolations of posterity. Small experimental theatres with low costs may hope to keep open while they educate their audiences, but the big theatres with big productions depend on giving the public what it will pay to see. Ellen Terry writing to Shaw expressed the dilemma: 'Now all the colour and warmth we get into Shakespeare plays would never, never (at this particular time) be (oh, I can't express what I mean), never be *made up for* to our audiences by substituting the tremendously powerful *bare* hardness of Ibsen's Borkman. As far as the Lyceum goes, it's much too big a theatre to play delicately any of Ibsen's modern plays.'

We should be careful before we are too scornful of melodrama. *Macbeth* and *Othello* are both melodrama although of exceptional quality. When we visit the theatre we accept in advance certain conventions. It is these conventions which vary from one generation to the other rather than the intellectual or artistic level. Many of the melodramas that Irving played were played for years after him by such actors as Sir John Martin Harvey and many had genuine power. Thus when Max Beerbohm saw *The Corsican Brothers* by Alexandre Dumas for the first time in 1908, although he wrote teasingly of the conventions of the play, he added: 'The solid fact remains that "*The Corsican Brothers*" really thrilled me, even moved me.'

When Ellen Terry joined the Lyceum company for the rehearsals of *Hamlet* she was surprised and disconcerted by the fact that Irving rehearsed every detail of the play except the scenes with Ophelia. As the first night drew near she went to him and begged him to rehearse her scenes.

'We shall be all right,' he replied, 'but we are not going to run the risk of being bottled up by a gasman or a fiddler.'

Irving had a real and lively admiration for her. Her pathos, he said, was 'nature helped by genius'. But on her first appearance at the Lyceum as Ophelia she felt that she had failed and she left the theatre as soon as she had finished her part, without waiting for the curtain calls. She drove up and down the Embankment in a cab for a long time until she felt the strength to go to her home in Longridge Road. Later that evening, so she told Marguerite Steen years afterwards, Irving, having missed her at the theatre, followed her to her house. There then began 'an attachment that lasted twenty years'.

Both Laurence Irving and Roger Manvell have been at great pains to establish the view, also held by members of the Terry family, that the love between Henry Irving and Ellen Terry was never consummated. This involves setting aside the evidence of Marguerite Steen, who reports the following conversation with Ellen Terry in her old age. 'The conversation had turned on some troublesome affair of my own, and led to my asking Ellen point-blank whether she had ever been Irving's mistress. She answered without hesitation: "Of course, I was. We were terribly in love for a while. Then, later on, when it didn't matter so much to me, he wanted us to go on, and so I did, because I was very, very fond of him and he said he needed me." ' Roger Manvell, quoting this conversation, says that he is inclined to think that 'she meant no more than that Irving and she were "lovers", and much together, but *not* that she had at any period actually *consummated* the relationship', a view which in its turn involves the belief that in her advanced age Ellen Terry was not aware of the precise meaning usually given to the word 'mistress'. She was at this time attempting to persuade Marguerite Steen to write about herself and the other Terrys.

The anxiety of the two biographers that their view of the matter should prevail may be because very few letters between the couple remain – suggesting that they regularly destroyed their correspondence and indicating a wish that their privacy might be respected. Nevertheless, a desire to preserve a secret that might be dangerous at the time does not completely establish a desire to keep the truth from posterity, while the very destruction of the letters – they both kept hundreds from other people – implies some special reason for it.

Possibly Irving's descendants have an inherited tendency to defend him against his wife. To other people it may seem natural and sympathetic that he should have had one complete relationship in his life. In all the thousands of words that have been written about him Irving so seldom emerges as a credible human being and, although this is partly because he deliberately built up a pontifical manner as a barrier between himself and the rest of the world, it is also because his personality has been obscured by the reverential manner with which writers have so often treated him. Yet there is evidence that he loved Ellen Terry and was prepared to risk a great deal for her. Laurence Irving says:

He believed, no doubt sincerely, that he loved her, and was prepared to sacrifice his jealously guarded independence for her sake. There was a time when he had hoped she might marry him – indeed he pressed her to do so. . . . Irving could not marry her unless his wife would agree to divorce him. If, in a moment of reckless passion, Irving had declared his readiness to suffer the indignity of a divorce case in which he would be the guilty party, she had been level-headed enough to count the cost, financially and artistically, of such a scandal – a scandal such as had ruined Edmund Kean. . . . He owed much to her intuitive wisdom.

There is also evidence to suggest a very intimate day-to-day relationship between the two. A slight but charming glimpse of her everyday life is given by D. S. MacColl, who lived opposite Ellen Terry in Longridge Road, and who with a single reference to Irving evokes a small, private world. He and his family were ignorant of the theatre and its stars, and, not recognising the actress, they dubbed her 'The Greek Lady'. He begins with a description of her departure for the theatre each day:

> She raised and kissed two little tots who were to be known as Edith and Gordon Craig. She greeted the next-door neighbours, family of a Rabbinical scholar, who had promptly become slaves of her apparition and stood ready on the pavement. Her cushions were brought out, placed and patted in the open carriage; herself installed; the air became tender and gay with wavings and blown kisses: the wheels revolved and greyness descended once more on Longridge Road.

The MacColl family, he then says, felt that the figure of Charles Kelly 'the manly bulldog sort of man', did not fit in with this 'Phantom of Delight' – he presented a false concord. 'When a year had passed that too substantial figure disappeared, and a new figure was seen in Longridge Road, spare and grim-jaunty, in close-fitting jacket, and tilted wide-a-wake; Henry Irving.'

And Gordon Craig, reciting a whimsical catalogue of Ellen Terry's doings during the week, ends: 'Saturday was always a half-holiday, spent in promising her advisers that she would be good next week – and on Sunday she generally drove away to Hampton Court with Irving, waving her lily white hand.' Then Laurence Irving says in a phrase which again suggests an intimate relationship: 'One Sunday evening Irving came to supper with Walter Pollock and his wife. Usually he brought Ellen Terry with him, but this time he came alone.' Most revealing of all, in Roger Manvell's biography we are given a few letters from Irving to Ellen Terry – of which with its splendid sense of ardour and urgency, the most attractive is:

Soon – Soon!
I shall be near you on Sunday.
God bless you my only thought.
Your own till Death.

And the most explicit: 'I am anxious to see Ted and hear of you. You gave me a lovely letter to take away with me on Monday. – My own dear wife as long as I live.' While in the only surviving letter she wrote him, she said: 'Dear – I'm better now and hope to come back to work tomorrow – I was dreadfully ill – but I struggled hard before I broke down – Thank you for *missing* me and for your loving letter. Your Nell.'

Behind the scenes at the Lyceum Theatre was the Old Beefsteak Club Room, built by Samuel Arnold, the composer, for the Sublime Society of Beefsteaks, of which Sheridan was a member. When Irving took over the management of the theatre he restored this room and the kitchen behind it. Here he entertained at supper after the theatre, finding at last an outlet for his hospitable nature and for his desire to relax over food and conversation after the strain of his performances. The Beefsteak Room served also as an ante-room when on special occasions, marking, for instance, the long run of a piece or a first night, Irving gave large parties on the specially decorated stage.

First nights were invariably treated as an occasion for hospittality, the large part of the audience consisting of Irving's invited guests. Among these, occupying the stage box, were always to be seen two boys with their mother – Irving's wife and sons. Florence Irving never relaxed the hatred and malice she felt for her husband, and she brought his sons up to regard their father with ridicule and contempt and Ellen Terry as the final insult to herself. They referred to their father as 'the Antique' and to his leading lady as 'the Wench'. But, in spite of her unrelenting spite, Mrs Irving never failed to appear at first nights in the place of honour as her husband's wife, and Laurence Irving suggests that to her hostile presence might be attributed the fact that Irving was then so often at his worst. Certainly he cannot have found much encouragement in the near presence of someone who on her return home on one occasion commented in her diary: 'First night of *Romeo and Juliet* at Lyceum – jolly failure – Irving awfully funny.'

Irving was a naturally hospitable man and the entertainments at the Lyceum were his greatest interest apart from his work. There are many descriptions of the parties in the Beefsteak Room but he himself moves through these a shadowy and lifeless figure. Few people penetrated the mystery of his personality when he was alive, none has left a vivid picture of him. His speeches were often written for him by other people and give no clue to his personality and, although Ellen Terry, at least, succeeds in conveying his personal appearance and physical charm, his recorded utterances, so often prefaced by the old actor's 'me boy', are mainly suggestive of the 'stock' character he himself did so much to outdate. Here once again Max Beerbohm, who scarcely knew him, has left a picture of him which has a natural authenticity.

He was always courteous and gracious. and everybody was fascinated by him; but I think there were few who did not also fear him. Always in the company of his friends and acquaintances —doubtless, not in that of his most intimate friends—there was an air of sardonic reserve behind his cordiality. He seemed always to be watching, and watching from a slight altitude. As when, on the first or last night of a play he made his speech before the curtain, and concluded by calling himself the public's 'respectful—devoted—loving—servant', with special emphasis on the word 'servant', he seemed always so like to some mighty cardinal stooping to wash the feet of pilgrims at the altar steps, so, when in private life people had the honour of meeting Irving, his exquisite manner of welcome stirred fear as well as love in their hearts. Irving, I think, wished to be feared as well as loved. He was 'a good fellow'; but he was also a man of genius, who had achieved pre-eminence in his art, and, thereby, eminence in the national life; and, naturally, he was not going to let the 'good fellow' in him rob him of the respect that was his due. Also, I think, the process of making himself feared appealed to something elfish in his nature. Remember, he was a comedian, as well as a tragedian. . . . He enjoyed the dignity of his position, but enjoyed even more, I conjecture, the fun of it.

Sir Mortimer Menpes also succeeds in a small but authentic glimpse of the actor, who sat to him for his portrait. One felt, he says, immediately one saw him, the 'generous soul of the man' – a remark that is saved from banality by the ring of truth. Irving had, no doubt, a nobility which was a part of his hold over audiences, and this was not diminished by a sardonic and slightly malicious humour of which Menpes gives an example. While he painted, Irving talked continuously, telling anecdotes and walking about illustrating them with mimicry. Once he described going in the company of Coquelin to see Tree play Falstaff.[8] Coquelin, he said, had been in constant fear that Tree would float right out of the theatre. 'Will he rise now?' he continually asked. 'Do you think he is going to rise?'

Irving had, in addition to a love of hospitality, a motive for the grand entertainments at the Lyceum to which he asked, as well as actors, writers and artists, the high society of London. He was concerned to raise the status of his profession and by acting as host to all the most influential people of the day he pursued an ambition only less important to him than his ambition as an actor.

In 1895, when Irving was fifty-seven and had been at the head of his profession for fifteen years or more, he gave a lecture at the Royal Institution of Great Britain. He began with a formal claim to have acting classified *officially* among the fine arts. He said: 'Official recognition of anything worthy is a good, or at least a useful thing. It is a part, and an important part, of the economy of the State: if it is not, of what use are titles and distinctions, names, badges, offices, in fact all the titular and sumptuary ways of distinction?'

Bernard Shaw, writing soon afterwards, said:

Here the 'formal claim' is put as precisely as Mr. Irving himself feels he can decorously put it. I, who am not an actor, and am therefore not hampered by any personal interest in the claim, can put it much more definitely. What Mr. Irving means us to answer is this question: 'The artist who composed the music for King Arthur is Sir Arthur Sullivan; the artist who composed the poem which made King Arthur known to this generation died Lord Tennyson; the artist who designed the suit of armour worn by King Arthur is

[8] Coquelin, Constant-Benoit, 1841–1909. Famous French actor and director, the original of Rostand's Cyrano de Bergerac.

Sir Edward Burne-Jones: why should the artist who plays King Arthur be only Mister Henry Irving?'

Henry Irving was indeed asking that, as leader of the theatrical profession, he should receive the same recognition as the leaders of other professions. It says a great deal for the integrity and single-mindedness of his purpose that no one at any time seems to have been astonished at this explicit and public claim to a knighthood or to have confused his motives with those of personal ambition. 'We owe him,' Bernard Shaw said, 'an unhesitating assumption that his jealousy is for the dignity of his art and not of himself, and that it would never have been advanced if the friend of Sir Joshua Reynolds had been Sir David Garrick, and if every successive P.R.A. had had for his officially recognised peer the leading actor of his day.'

On 24 May 1895, a few weeks after he made this speech, Irving received two letters. The first, from Lord Rosebery, told him that the Queen had conferred on him the honour of a knighthood, and the second brought him the congratulations of the Prince of Wales. Thus for the first time in history acting was officially recognised as an art.

We owe to the occasion on which he received his knighthood, and once more to Max Beerbohm, one of the most charming of all the rare peeps behind his pontifical manner. Crossing the road opposite Marble Arch Beerbohm saw Irving in a brougham on his way to Paddington to take the train to Windsor Castle.

Irving [he says] in his most prelatical mood, had always a touch – a trace here and there – of the old Bohemian. But as I caught sight of him on this occasion . . . he was the old Bohemian and nothing else. His hat was tilted at more than its usual angle, and his long cigar seemed longer than ever: and on his face was a look of such ruminant, sly fun as I have never seen equalled. I had but a moment's glimpse of him; but that was enough to show me the soul of a comedian revelling in the part he was about to play – of a comedic philosopher revelling in a foolish world. I was sure that when he alighted on the platform of Paddington station his bearing would be more than ever grave and stately, with even the usual touch of Bohemianism obliterated now in honour of the honour that was to befall him.

Irving made his first tour in America in 1883. It had been customary for many years for English and American actors to cross the Atlantic and appear in London or New York, as the case might be, as visiting stars. Because of the dearth of playwrights in the English language both countries relied heavily on the classics and the French for their plays, so that visitors to either had to stand comparison with the greatest actors of the past in roles that were equally well-known to both. Irving, however, took with him not merely the whole Lyceum company but the Lyceum productions and he introduced to the United States an entirely new conception of theatrical production.

He was accompanied throughout the tour by Joseph Hatton, who was there to write a record of it. In *Henry Irving's Impressions of America* Hatton has left a charming account of the arrival in New York harbour of the *Britannic* carrying Irving, Ellen Terry and the rest of the company. Although the ship arrived in the early hours of the morning it was met by two yachts – one carrying the impresario who had arranged the tour and thirty serenading Italian musicians, the other carrying the famous actors Lawrence Barrett and William Florence. Irving and Ellen Terry were immediately transferred to the yacht *Blackbird*, where they encountered for the first time that typically American phenomenon, the 'interviewer'. At four o'clock in the morning a party of journalists had left New York to meet the *Britannic* and put Irving and Ellen Terry through the customary and much advertised 'grilling' – an ordeal the couple had awaited with some fear since leaving England's shores. The ease with which Irving talked to these journalists did a great deal to assure the success of his visit.

'Now gentlemen,' he said, in the prolonged silence which greeted his arrival among them, 'time flies. . . . I have a dread of you. Don't ask me how I like America at present – I shall, I am sure; and I think the bay superb. There, I place myself at your mercy. Don't spare me.'

And when asked what he did for exercise, he replied: 'I act.'

In New York, although well treated by the newspapers and royally entertained he was made very nervous before his first night by the activity of the ticket speculators. In New York speculators in theatre tickets are protected by the law and managers are obliged to sell to them. These dealers, if they can persuade the public to pay, can double or treble the price of the tickets, making as much out of a great success as the management of the theatre and, as Irving feared, putting the holders of tickets into a highly critical mood. On the advice of William Winter, a New York critic, Irving had decided to open with *The Bells*. Winter had said that Irving and his audience would be in a mood of great excitement on the first night and that it would be best to take advantage of this agitation to play the exacting part in which he had made his name, which would also allow him to avoid comparison with any established favourite. It had the disadvantage, however, of having no part for Ellen Terry.

From the moment Irving, dressed as Matthias, appeared on the stage with the cry: 'It is I!' the success of the Lyceum tour was assured. James Hatton tells us that, interviewed in his dressing room at the end of the play, he was asked whether he felt he had been judged on his merits, whether there was any trace of independence in the manner of the audience.

'Yes, yes, – there was certainly,' said the actor, rising and pacing the room. 'It is not presumption in me to say that I am sure I was judged solely on my merits, and that the audience went away pleased with me. There were times tonight when I could feel the sympathy of my hearers – actually feel it.'

And asked later: 'Do you look upon your reception tonight as a success?' he replied:

'In every way. One of your greatest actors told me that American audiences are proverbially cold on first nights. He was trying to save me from a possible disappointment. In addition to this "The Bells" is not a play for applause, but for earnest, sympathetic silence. Need I say that the demonstrations which burst forth on every occasion that good taste would allow, are the best evidence that to-night I have won an artistic triumph.'

The following morning the New York newspapers confirmed the impressions of the actor, and on the following night, as Henrietta Maria in *Charles I*, Ellen Terry made an almost equal success.

In New York Irving presented in addition *Louis XI*, *The Merchant of Venice*, *The Lyons Mail* and *The Belle's Stratagem*, reserving *Hamlet* for the more intellectual audience of

Philadelphia and *Much Ado About Nothing* for Chicago, and playing both on a return visit to New York. At the end of his first tour of Boston, Baltimore, Chicago, St Louis, Cincinnati, Columbus, Washington and the larger towns of New England a little over 400,000 dollars had been paid direct to the theatres to see him, of which he received a half share. His profit on the whole enterprise was £11,700.

Irving and the Lyceum company returned to America in the following autumn of 1885 and, starting in Quebec, toured in North America for seven months. George Alexander was in this company, having taken the place of William Terriss, and also John Martin Harvey. In view of the success of the first tour Irving had decided to arrange and manage the second one himself. As a result he this time cleared a profit of £15,000 out of takings of £80,000. Laurence Irving remarks that this was a great thing for Irving, who 'could foresee that by touring periodically in the provinces of England and the United States he could endow the Lyceum so handsomely that he could maintain his ever-increasing establishment and be free to experiment as he chose without undue risk.' This was a slightly optimistic view of the ultimate requirements of the Lyceum, but it did not over-estimate the importance for the rest of his life of Irving's popularity in America.

In 1892 Edmund Yates, the editor of a fashionable weekly called *The World*, gave his musical critic a letter he had received from Ellen Terry asking his advice on a young 'composer-singer friend of mine'. As a result there began a correspondence which is among the most famous and extraordinary ever written. It is extraordinary because for years Bernard Shaw and Ellen Terry never met and, when they did, saw each other only occasionally on business. It was a love affair on paper and, if one examines the other relationships of this pair with the opposite sex, one cannot help feeling it was ideally suited to both – engaging their desire to love and be loved and their talents for letter-writing, while excluding the need to evade greater demands. The correspondence did not completely come to an end until late in Ellen Terry's life, but it was in the 1890s that it was at its height. In 1896 the couple wrote to each other on average every four days and in 1897 every three.

D

Their correspondence is relevant here only where it touches the life of Henry Irving. Roger Manvell says that the love between Irving and Ellen Terry began to cool in the middle nineties and, although this process may have begun before the correspondence with Bernard Shaw, there is no doubt that Irving was hurt and bewildered by his leading lady's friendship with one of his leading critics. Shaw railed incessantly at Irving in the press, because – he was later to say – having marked Irving when young as the actor for the new theatre in which he was interested and Ellen Terry as the actress, he could never forgive him for wasting his own and Ellen Terry's talents in old-fashioned melodramas and what he described as 'costly Bardicide'. In fact Shaw was completely cold to Irving's romantic school of acting, although he wasted a great deal of energy in an attempt to persuade Irving to put on one of his own plays, but he adored Ellen Terry. This was bad enough when criticism of the actor-manager combined with praise of his leading lady were merely a regular feature of notices of the Lyceum productions, but it must have seemed incredible to Irving that Ellen Terry should condone the process Bernard Shaw afterwards described in the following terms: 'I destroyed her belief in him and gave shape and consciousness to her sense of having her possibilities sterilized by him.'

In an analysis of the character of Desdemona Ellen Terry, having remarked that she is 'genially expressive', wrote: 'The pertinacity with which she begs Othello to reinstate Cassio does not strike me as evidence that she is a rather foolish woman. . . . Her purity of heart and her charity (charity "thinketh no evil") are sufficient explanation of her being slow to grasp the situation.'

This might be a description of Ellen Terry herself. She was not a stupid woman but she badgered Irving about Shaw – begging him to put on *The Man of Destiny*, quoting Shaw's views, working to bring about a meeting between the two and so on – and in the accounts of these conversations written to Shaw there is no suggestion that she felt any compunction, anything except an honourable sense of doing her duty towards Irving.

We know very little of Irving's side of this matter but we do know that he referred to Shaw as Mr Pshaw and he told his son Laurence that he would 'cheerfully have paid Shaw's funeral expenses at any time.'

That in fact Ellen Terry's deep feeling for Irving was never weakened by her flirtatious relationship with Shaw is proved in a letter written to Shaw in 1897. 'If you worry (or try to worry) Henry I must end our long and close friendship. He is ill, and what would I not do to better him?'

However, Bernard Shaw apart, Irving and Ellen Terry were by now beginning to turn away from each other for the satisfaction of their emotional needs. Their biographers once more are inclined to pass over this period of their lives, and in everything written about them there is only a sentence or two that breaks an otherwise complete silence on the subject. If these sentences seem here to be seized upon, it is not only because of their rarity but also because of their meaning, which, while it attaches to trivial things, is nevertheless unequivocal. The first occurs in Laurence Irving and concerns the year 1896. 'Tongues', he says, 'had begun to wag over Ellen Terry's undisguised partially for Frank Cooper.'⁹ The second sentence occurs in one of Ellen Terry's letters to Bernard Shaw, dated 18 January 1898. 'Henry,' she says, 'is so nice to me lately that I'm convinced he has a new "flame" (he is always nicer then, which I think is to his credit).' Henry had, in fact, met someone whose importance to him was to be much greater than that of a new 'flame', and a month later Ellen Terry, again writing to Bernard Shaw, asked: 'But who is Mrs Aria? I only know she is "a journalist" and "a friend" of H.I.s. I never set eyes on her and she has no idea I know of her. (This is fun, and would be better fun, if I knew something about her.) If you know her personally don't "give away" that I know of her existence.'

In answer to the question: 'Who is Mrs Aria?' Bernard Shaw replied that as far as he could judge she was 'a good sort'. Years later Marguerite Steen brought a book of Mrs Aria's to

⁹ Frank Cooper was an actor who played Laertes at the Lyceum and now returned to play Modred in *King Arthur*. On 11 June 1897 Bernard Shaw wrote to Ellen Terry: 'Cooper is quite a pretty, amiable-looking, chubby fellow off the stage, with a complexion as charming as wig paste. Perhaps it *is* wig paste. Why can't he be taught to act? Has he NO intelligence?' But in October of the same year Ellen Terry wrote to a friend: 'No – I fear I can't snap up Frank Cooper (!) and marry him, for he happens to have a wife – and she's nice too – so he can't "cut her throat with a bar of soap" – She is a jealous little lady too, but *not* of me – and I'm fond of her. They marry me to every man I act with.'

Ellen Terry because it contained a study of Henry Irving. She writes:

Ellen Terry glanced at the title and the name of the author and laid the book quietly aside.

'Thank you, my dear. . . . Henry left me for Mrs. Aria.'

And Marguerite Steen adds: 'After twenty years that wound still ached.'

Mrs Aria was, in fact, the solace of Henry Irving's last years and she describes her friendship with him in a book entitled *My Sentimental Self*. She is described by Laurence Irving as 'educated by the conversation of Labby, Wilde, George Moore and their satellites', and as 'the Récamier of Regent's Park – rarely leaving a chaise-longue round which literary tigers like Courtney, Wells, Arnold Bennett and George Moore purred in happy competition.' But she is unskilled with the pen and in her memoirs assumes a degree of piety towards Irving which today is distasteful. The witch, Ellen Terry, possessed of all the talents, has no difficulty in retaining our sympathies over the years. That she was at this time in need of them is suggested in the remark by which Roger Manvell introduces sentences from her private diary, reflecting on Irving as a man and an actor. 'This splendid analysis,' he says, 'is warm, yet accurate, and most courageous in the face of what Ellen realised she must be losing as his affections moved elsewhere.'

As Irving's sons grew up they gradually established a relationship with him. This was delayed by the hatred they had been brought up to feel for Ellen Terry, whom they still referred to as the Wench, and by the desire of both to go on the stage, which he opposed. They had been encouraged by their mother, in a purely amateur way, in careers as child actors and they seem in their youth to have suffered from the idea, often held by children of the very talented, that the world which their father had made available to himself was in part available to them. They resented the fact that even when he consented to their theatrical ambitions he would not immediately help them to leading parts. They resented to the presence of Edward Gordon Craig in the Lyceum company. In 1891 Laurence wrote to his brother as follows: 'I cannot say I was astonished at Irving being at Malvern with Terry. I might have been had he been there without Terry. We are cutting ourselves adrift from the old hulk and very soon we shall not need to fear his hatred or win his love. That he could not take us into his company was true whilst he is stuffing the goose with bastards of the fell Terry breed.' And soon after: 'Irving was very dull. He was so icy and obnoxious. I was glad to leave him to himself.'

In the end it was Ellen Terry's genuine admiration for Laurence as a playwright and her interest in his career in the theatre as much as anything else which finally brought him, and following him Harry, into a real relationship with their father. By 1898 after the production by his father of his play *Peter the Great*, Laurence is writing to him: 'I can't tell you how full my heart was and is of admiration and gratitude. . . . Your exquisite judgment has guided the play safely into harbour so far and I can rely on it implicitly. Best Love. "My father is great. I am proud to be his son." ' And when Harry discovered that his mother's family had used the occasion of his marriage to work themselves into a frenzy of conjecture as to whether Ellen Terry would accompany Irving to the wedding, he wrote to Dorothea Baird:

I am sorry all this E.T. business is cropping up again in South Kensington. How wretched it is! I had hoped they would have spared you all unpleasantness. Whatever the whole business means my father is now at an age when the matter may surely be set at rest, and the family linen not washed to every newcomer. Heaven knows it is distressing enough to Laurence and myself to be planted in the midst of all this scandal and we have done our best to steer some sort of course between it. And why all this excitement? I don't anticipate any trouble from E.T. She is not so blind or foolish as yet.

You will have to meet her as I met her and be rather bored by her, but she will not want to come to the wedding or to our house or do anything that might be inconvenient.

In the end Irving himself refused to go to the wedding but he joined his son and his bride at Bamburgh during their honeymoon. From this time both sons were more or less fully reconciled to their father, Laurence eventually becoming a member of the Lyceum company.

Irving had a splendid unconcern with money and, like so many people who do not care for it, he needed a great deal in order to do as he wished in the realm of the things he did care for. The productions at the Lyceum were never stinted of anything needed to complete the beauty or authenticity of the effects aimed at. They continued to draw the public and this lavishness might not have been fatal if the henchmen, so devoted in many ways, had included among them a good business manager. But the discipline which was so notable a feature of the artistic sphere at the Lyceum did not extend to the financial departments. The number of camp followers grew and abuse of Irving's generosity infected almost every part of the theatre. Money was wasted and misappropriated.

In December 1896, after the first night of a revival of *Richard III*, Irving slipped on the narrow stairs of his flat and ruptured the ligatures of his knee. Ellen Terry was away in Germany and the Lyceum had to be closed for a week. *Cymbeline* was revived with Julia Arthur as Imogen and later with Ellen Terry herself. The play covered only about 25 per cent of the costs. *Olivia* was then tried and ran at only a small loss to the end of the season. It was then discovered that £10,000 had been lost and it became clear on how narrow a margin the Lyceum company operated. Handsome profits on the autumn tour enabled Irving to forget the situation for a while.

Then in February of the following year a disaster occurred. Over the past twenty years a great store of scenery and properties had been acquired, much of it the work of the greatest scenic artists of the day. This was Irving's capital, and the basis on which he had operated a policy to withdraw plays before their attraction was exhausted so that these successful productions might, in London, but more especially in the provinces and America, take care of his declining years. All this property was under-insured – quite recently the insurance had been reduced in an effort towards economy – and when the buildings in which it was stored were burned down and with them 260 scenes – the settings for forty-four plays – £6,000 was all that remained of the accumulation of a lifetime.

Irving is said to have taken this disaster with great philosophy and courage, and once more he took to the provinces to restore some of his fallen fortunes. On his way to a train one night he got his feet wet before a journey in an unheated carriage. By the end of the week he was suffering from pneumonia and pleurisy and again it was demonstrated that the star system requires the star. By the end of a tour in which the profit was only £500, Bram Stoker, his business manager, was forced to let the Lyceum and arrange a further provincial tour for the company.

Irving's finances were by now so reduced that in order to tide himself over his illness he was forced to sell most of his collection of theatrical books and prints and, for the first time since he had ceased to be a provincial actor, to borrow from friends. In the circumstances the step he now took was more or less forced upon him, although the arrangements made should have been more favourable to him. For certain immediate financial considerations and against the advice of his own staff he engaged himself to a company to be called the Lyceum Theatre Company, on terms which made it possible for it to make a profit at the same time as he made a loss. At the end of the first season he had lost £4,000 while making a large profit for the company. He had never recovered from the effects of pneumonia, which left him with a chronic inflammation of the throat, but he now undertook an extensive tour of the provinces followed by a long tour through Canada and America. The takings of this tour were £111,000 and although this was no greater than the takings of previous tours, the Lyceum Company on this occasion justified itself by taking out of it four times as much profit, on which Irving's share was £24,000.

During this tour he and Ellen Terry discussed for the first time the possibility of her ceasing to play with him. She was by now fifty-two and the range of parts in Irving's repertoire suitable to a woman of that age was naturally becoming narrow. This difficulty might somehow have been overcome but for the fact that their relationship had become one in which it was possible for them to contemplate parting. Laurence Irving says of Irving at this time: 'The last two years had had their effect upon his outward bearing; a shield of cynicism concealed his bruised pride; an affection of republicanism, the refuge of the dethroned autocrat, tempered his austerity. He evaded a difficult decision and was more tolerant of the incompetence of others. In short, he was a sick man.'

In the same year Ellen Terry wrote to Bernard Shaw: 'Ah, I feel so certain Henry just hates me! I can only *guess* at it, for he is exactly the same sweet-mannered person he was when "I felt so certain" Henry loved me! We have not met for years now, except before other people, where my conduct exactly matches his of course. All my own fault. It is *I* am changed, not he. It's all right, but it has squeezed me up dreadfully.' But she was also rebellious of Irving's management and contemplating leaving him. Before the American tour she had written to Shaw:

When I come back I shall probably *be quite* a year younger, and if H.I. gives me only half a fairly good part, I shall play it, but if a part is offered me like the kind of thing I did (or didn't) in *Peter the Great*, *Medicine Man* or *Robespierre* I shall 'refuse to act' (for the first time in my life) and give it all up and come and settle quietly in a place like this and perhaps act sometimes, on occasions when I could fit in better than another. I should never say good-bye. Just leave off.

However, neither Irving nor Ellen Terry was ultimately yet prepared to make the break. Laurence Irving says that Irving 'would not scruple to use every subtle inducement to keep her at his side', while Ellen Terry could still write to Shaw: 'I appear to be of strange *use* to H., and I have always thought to be useful, really useful, to any one person *is* rather fine and satisfactory.'

Between 1894 and 1900 Ellen Terry made notes in a diary 'About H.I.' In 1895 she wrote the following description of him.

A splendid figure. and his face very noble. A superb brow: rather small dark eyes which can at moments become immense, and hang like a bowl of dark liquid, with light shining through; a most refined curving Roman nose, strong and delicate in line. and *cut clean* (as all his features); a smallish mouth, and full of the most wonderful teeth, even at 55; lips most delicate and refined – firm, firm, firm – and with a rare smile of the most exquisite beauty, and quite-not-to-be described kind. (He seems almost ashamed of his smile, even in very private life, and will withdraw it at once in public.) His chin, and the line from ear to chin is firm, extremely delicate, and very strong and clean defined. He has an ugly ear! Large, flabby, ill-cut, and pasty-looking, pale and lumpy. His hair is superb: beautiful in 1867, when I first met him, when it was blue-black like a raven's wing, it is even more splendid now (1895) when it is liberally streaked with white. . . . Never have I seen such hands, 'in form and moving how *express* and admirable'. He always makes them up for the stage very brown.

In 1896 she wrote:

H.I. is much handsomer now than when I first knew him in 1867. Handsomer, but somehow more furtive looking. . . . If it could be possible for him to take infinite pains for another, he would be a perfect being, but self-concentration spoils the porridge.
Indifference is personified in H.I.

In 1897 she wrote:

Very odd. He is not improving with age.

And in 1898:

For years he has accepted favours, obligations to, etc., *through* Bram Stoker! Never will he acknowledge them himself, either by business-like receipt or by any word or sign.

In 1899 she wrote an account of a visit she paid him in Bournemouth where he was recovering from a serious illness. After remarking that 'poor old King H.' was at his 'downest' she goes on to say that she is amazed at the few in number of his useful friends. 'He wanted to tell me that not only was he broken in health but he was what is called "ruined". At which words I refused to shed tears, for, I said: "As long as you and I have health, we have means of wealth. We can pack a bag, each of us and trot round the Provinces. Yes, and go to America, Australia, India, Japan." ' To her astonishment Irving replied that the reason he had asked her to come to see him was to tell her that he was already arranging a tour of the English provinces with a small company playing *The Bells, Louis XI* and *A Story of Waterloo* – all plays in which there was no part for her.

'*What* plays?' she asked, and 'Where do I come in?' and she says that Irving looked exceedingly silly when he replied that as there was no chance of acting at the Lyceum 'you can, of course, er, *do as you like*'.

'I felt,' she writes, 'a good many feelings. At the top of all came amusement to save the situation. Then,' said I, 'I have in plain terms what Ted would call "the dirty kick out"?'

But, if it was the 'dirty kick out', it was at this time only temporary. In the following year, as has been seen, she was back and touring in the provinces and in America with him.

Nevertheless, the glorious days were over and in front only the steady decline. When Irving returned from America he was informed that the London County Council, which had embarked on a policy of enforcement of safety regulations against fire, required alterations to the Lyceum Theatre which would cost £20,000. This ultimatum caused the company, an 'over-capitalised concern built on the quivering sands of theatrical speculation' to close the theatre and call in the Receiver. This was a very bitter blow to Irving.

At the end of the Lyceum season of 1902, both this great theatre, so long a feature of the London scene, and the most famous partnership in theatrical history came to an end when Irving led Ellen Terry forward to acknowledge the applause after a performance of *The Merchant of Venice*. They played together once more at an all-star matinée in aid of the Actors' Benevolent Fund, and they did not formally part until she refused to accompany him to America in an absurd play about Dante by Sardou, on which he had already lost a great deal of money at the Theatre Royal, Drury Lane. Irving then left for America without her.

They were to meet only once more. Irving's popularity was so great both in Britain and America that it was true, as she had told him at Bournemouth, that as long as he had health he could have continued to earn money touring with a few old plays. But his health was rapidly failing. In 1905 he was so ill at Wolverhampton that his company had to be disbanded in the middle of a tour. Ellen Terry then travelled at once to see him.

I found him sitting up in bed, drinking his coffee. He looked like some beautiful grey tree that I have seen in Savannah. His old dressing-gown hung about his frail yet majestic figure like some mysterious grey drapery. We were both very much moved, and said little. 'I'm glad you've come. Two Queens have been kind to me this morning. Queen Alexandra telegraphed to say how sorry she was I was ill, and now you – '.

Irving never recovered his health. He continued to tour but it became more and more obvious that he was a sick man struggling to carry on. In Bradford in the same year, 1905, he appeared in *Becket* in which the last lines he spoke were: 'Into thy hands, O Lord, into thy hands!' He left the theatre alone with his valet and died in the hall of his hotel.

Like so many actors before him, he died penniless. His pictures, theatrical relics, clothes and properties were sold to provide for his only dependant, his widow. He was buried in Westminster Abbey under a pall of laurel leaves and he entered immediately into his posthumous reputation.

Sir George Alexander
1858-1918

George Alexander secured a place in the annals of the theatre by what at first sight seems to be an extraordinary instinct for the historical occasion.

He was born on 19 June 1858 at Reading and named George Alexander Gibb Samson. His father had an agency in the dry-goods trade and he received most of his education at the High School of Stirling. He left school at the age of fifteen to become a clerk in a London office and at this time he took part at least once a year in amateur dramatic performances. Then in 1879, at the expense of a total, although, as it turned out, only temporary breach with his father, he dropped the last two of his four names and joined a stock company at the Theatre Royal, Nottingham. His rise was very rapid and two years later he was engaged by Henry Irving to play Caleb Deecie in a revival of Albery's comedy *The Two Roses* at the Lyceum. Following this he had an engagement with Hare and Kendal at the St James's Theatre and then he returned to the Lyceum Company where he remained for six years.

Alexander was a very good-looking man with a good figure and excellent legs – a dandy and the original matinée idol. In a belittling and rather too much quoted sentence, Henry Irving is supposed to have said to him at rehearsal one day: 'Now Alexander, not quite so much Piccadilly.' However, in spite of a natural propensity for 'too much Piccadilly' he was a very good actor who during his six years at the Lyceum learned his trade the hard way. He is quoted as saying: 'When I was at the Lyceum, after five or six hours of rehearsal by Irving I would go home almost crying. I would tell my wife that I was afraid

I had made a dreadful mistake in going on the stage. And I made up my mind that if I ever had a company of my own, I would let them down pretty easy.'

Alexander went to America with the Lyceum company and in Boston, where Irving developed a painful swelling of the leg, he had to go on as Benedick at a few hours notice and with an imperfect knowledge of the lines. In London he took William Terriss's place in the company, his most notable role being that of Faust.

In 1889, there being no part for him in the Lyceum production of *The Amber Heart*, he accepted an engagement at the Adelphi with the Gattis. During this period he took a short lease of the Avenue Theatre and put on a play called *Dr Bill*. Because the Gattis would not release him to act in it, he engaged Fred Terry to play the part he might have played himself.[1] Then in 1890, against the advice of Henry Irving, who told him that he could return to the Lyceum after six months if he wished to, he signed a lease for the St James's Theatre, installed electric light there, re-upholstered the seats and started his long career as an actor-manager.

Alexander, like Bancroft, was a naturally shrewd administrator and much of his success at the St James's can be attributed to the efficiency of his management of the theatre. A large part of it was due, however, to his policy of promoting the work of British playwrights. He was the first to recognise that in the new prosperity and status of the theatre writers of the highest quality might be persuaded to work in it. He suggested to men who had never thought of writing a play that they might consider doing so, and he invited them to bring ideas to him so that the dramatic possibilities might be discussed in advance. He had chosen his moment correctly and his policy brought him success: he produced sixty-two full length plays and nineteen one-act plays in twenty-seven years of management, and only eight of these were of foreign origin.

It was this policy rather than some uncanny flair that made his period at the St James's memorable in the history of the theatre.

---

[1] Terry, Fred, 1863–1933. Ellen Terry's brother. In the Bancroft company and played Sebastian to Ellen Terry's Viola at the Lyceum. Chiefly remembered as Sir Percy Blakeney in *The Scarlet Pimpernel*.

On 20 February 1892, just over a year after he had opened in management at the St James's, Alexander put on the first of the plays for which he is remembered. This was *Lady Windermere's Fan*, for which he had paid an advance of royalties of £100 before a line or even a scenario was written. When he first read the play he offered to buy it for £1,000, but Wilde replied: 'I have so much confidence in your excellent judgment, my dear Aleck, that I cannot but refuse your generous offer.' And in fact Wilde made £7,000 out of royalties from the original run.

Lady Windermere's Fan conforms to the stage conventions of the time and is distinguishable from dozens of other comedies only because of the talent, wit and wisdom of the dialogue. As an actor-manager Alexander gave far more consideration to the views of his playwrights and the casting of supporting roles than did, for instance, Irving, but he was master of his own theatre and well aware of his own importance to any play produced in it. It was not to be expected that he and Wilde would reach the first performance of this play without some differences of opinion, but all the evidence suggests that most of Alexander's proposed alterations were finally accepted by the author because they were genuine improvements on the original text.

One of these alterations was merely the interpolation of two lines at the end of Act 2. Mrs Erlynne, before rushing off to find her daughter, instructs Lord Augustus Lorton to take Lord Windermere to his club and keep him there as long as possible. Originally the Act-drop followed immediately on the following speech:

Mrs Erlynne: Don't let Windermere out of your sight tonight. If you do I will never forgive you. I will never speak to you again. I'll have nothing to do with you. Remember you are to keep Windermere at your club, and don't let him come back to-night.

Alexander wanted a different ending and suggested to Wilde that two lines should be added.

Lord Augustus: Well, really, I might be her husband already. Positively I might. (*Follows her in a bewildered manner.*)

A second alteration was of greater importance. Originally

the secret that Mrs Erlynne is Lady Windermere's mother was kept until the last act. Alexander felt, in the words of his biographer, 'that to allow the audiences to remain unaware of the reason for Lord Windermere's submission to the demands of Mrs Erlynne for the greater part of the play and then with a sharp twist to let them into the secret, would introduce a trickiness quite alien from and probably fatal to the success of the play. *Lady Windermere's Fan* would become a riddle long drawn out, instead of a play of real emotion and suspense.'

The request for these alterations produced a letter from Wilde in which he complained that the first of the two had been made in his absence 'through illness caused by the worry and anxiety I have gone through at the theatre', but said that, although the new ending came as a shock of surprise, he did not in any degree object to it. And he added plaintively: 'To reproach me on Wednesday for not having written a speech for a situation on which I was not consulted and of which I was quite unaware was, of course, a wrong thing to do.'

He was much more upset by the suggestion for the second alteration, and wrote:

With regard to your other suggestion about the disclosure of the secret of the play in the second act, had I intended to let out the secret, which is the element of suspense and curiosity, a quality so essentially dramatic, I would have written the play on entirely different lines. I would have made Mrs Erlynne a vulgar, horrid woman and struck out the incident of the fan. The audience must not know till the last act that the woman Lady Windermere proposed to strike with her fan was her own mother. The note would be too harsh, too horrible.

Writing of this incident, A. E. W. Mason says: 'Wilde gave way in the end, which suggests that he gave way to pressure from Alexander. But the play seems to have had its first performance with the sequence unchanged and six days afterwards Wilde wrote to the editor of the St James's Gazette asking permission to correct a statement put forward 'in your issue of this evening' to the effect that he had made the alteration in consequence of the newspaper criticisms.

The facts are as follows. On last Saturday night, after the play was over, and the author, cigarette in hand, had delivered a delightful and immortal speech, I had the pleasure of entertaining at supper a small number of personal friends: and, as none of them was older than myself, I naturally listened to their artistic views with attention and pleasure. The opinions of the old on matters of Art are, of course, of no value whatsoever. The artistic instincts of the young are invariably fascinating.

He goes on to say that the opinion of his friends was that the psychological interest of the second act of the play would be greatly increased by the disclosure of the actual relationship existing between Lady Windermere and Mrs Erlynne, 'an opinion I may add, that had previous been strongly held and urged by Mr Alexander'. 'This determination, however, was entered into long before I had the opportunity of studying the culture, courtesy and critical faculty displayed by such papers as the *Referee*, *Reynolds*, and the *Sunday Sun*.'

On 27 May 1893 Alexander produced *The Second Mrs Tanqueray* by Arthur W. Pinero. In the course of time Pinero has come to be regarded as a good craftsman but not a great artist, a playwright with a strong dramatic sense but one whose characters speak a stilted, rather pretentious dialogue and are moved in improbable situations by artificial emotions.[2] But the first night of *The Second Mrs Tanqueray* was a great theatrical occasion. Mrs Tanqueray is a woman with a 'past' – by which in this case is meant that she has had physical inter-course with men in return for money – who, as the second wife of a country gentleman, is attempting to forget it. During the course of the play it is discovered that her step-daughter's fiancé has formerly been her lover and in the last act she commits suicide. The novelty and the daring of presenting such a woman on the stage was confused, as daring so often is, with truth and naturalness. William Archer wrote:

It is not merely or mainly superior gifts, then, but superior strength of character, which has given this victory to Mr Pinero rather than to Mr Oscar Wilde, Mr Henry Arthur Jones, Mr Grundy or Mr Carton. Any difference of endowment between him and them is not sufficient to account for the immense difference between

[2] Pinero's virtues, particularly as a writer of farce, should not be underrated, however. *The Second Mrs Tanqueray*, *Trelawny of the Wells* and *The Magistrate* have all been revived in the 1960s and welcomed by the critics – the last named being thought to stand comparison with Feydeau's farces.

The Second Mrs Tanqueray and the very best work of any of these writers. It is the attitude of mind in which he approached his task, the artistic ideal he proposed to himself, and his unflinching devotion to that ideal, that have enabled him to produce the one play of what may be called European merit which the modern English stage can as yet boast.

The first night of *The Second Mrs Tanqueray* is famous not only for the emergence of a new dramatist who seemed of 'European' quality but of the young actress who played Paula Tanqueray. There had been difficulty in casting the part. Olga Nethersole, Janet Achurch and Winifred Emery had all been suggested and Elizabeth Robins actually engaged, but when after some reluctance the Gatti brothers agreed to release Mrs Patrick Campbell from her contract with them, Miss Robins resigned in favour of the younger woman. Mrs Patrick Campbell's success in the play is part of theatrical history. So, too, are her quarrels with Alexander. She became notorious for the havoc she caused in the theatre through a mixture of caprice and moodiness, a liking for practical joking and a sharp tongue. Hesketh Pearson wrote of her that she ruined Alexander's natural good temper and was the occasion of hysteria and heat, bawling and disputing in his normally beautifully run theatre. She herself says that once she and Alexander rehearsed 'only addressing each other in the words of our parts'. And on another occasion:

Mr Alexander in this play by Mr Jones had to look into my face and tell me I was beautiful and that he adored me, or some such words. And one night he said it with such a look in his eyes, as though he would willingly have wrung my neck, that I burst out laughing. When the curtain fell, his stage-manager came with pompous dignity to the door of my dressing-room and said, 'Mr Alexander's compliments and will you please not laugh at him on the stage.' I replied, 'My compliments to Mr Alexander, and please tell him I never laugh at him until I get home.'

The Second Mrs Tanqueray ran for nearly a year and was followed by *The Masqueraders*, an almost equally successful play by Henry Arthur Jones. During the run of *The Second Mrs Tanqueray* Henry James had completed *Guy Domville*, which he had agreed to write for Alexander, and it caused him much pain when he had to wait for the whole of the long run of Henry Arthur Jones's play before his own could be produced.

James's attitude to the theatre was ambivalent. He had for long been drawn to the dramatic form but he had a very low opinion of the theatre in London. His unrestrained, even vicious criticism of the work of other people and his sensitive, almost craven concern for his own show him, unusually, in an unsympathetic light. Elizabeth Robins, who sometimes accompanied him to the theatre, wrote: 'One never grew wholly acclimatised to the nipping airs that now and then would blow about the startled stalls. Mr James's all too audible remarks, conveyed in terms always "chosen", often singularly picturesque, sometimes diabolic, as though he revelled in mercilessness – would send cold shivers down his companion's spine.' And his biographer says:

He was attracted to the theatre and at the same time was repelled by it. He wanted its successes and rewards and yet was afraid to chance its pitfalls. . . . When a magazine rejected a story – this was a private matter between editor and writer. But when a play was announced, publicized, promised to the public, and then not produced, or failed in production, the author was, in the process, publicly rejected. This was what Henry James feared more than anything else.

In 1888, after the unappreciative reception of *The Bostonians* and, following that, of *The Princess Casamassima*, James received an invitation from Edward Compton, a young actor-manager whose company toured the provinces, to dramatise *The American*. James said sometimes that he was influenced by the comparatively large income made by playwrights such as Pinero and Wilde and at other times he confessed to an almost lifelong temptation to write for the theatre. He accepted the invitation. 'Don't be hard on me,' he wrote to Robert Louis Stevenson, 'simplifying and chastening necessity has laid its brutal hand on me and I have had to try and make somehow or other the money I don't make by literature.' And speaking of a rehearsal he is about to attend as 'a base theatrical errand', he also wrote: 'My zeal in the affair is only matched by my indifference.' But at the same time he was writing to his brother William: 'I feel at last as if I had found my *real* form, which

I am capable of carrying far, and for which the pale little art of fiction, as I have practised it, has been, for me, but a limited and restricted substitute.'

The American, after playing successfully in the provincial towns, was brought to London, where it ran sufficiently well for James to be able to write: 'Honour is saved, but I grieve to say nothing else, for the piece made no money.'

Soon after this he saw Alexander's production of *The Second Mrs Tanqueray* and he felt that he had 'at last found a manager for whom he could do a serious play'. He discussed three different ideas with Alexander but finally sent him the first act and the scenario for two more acts of the play which became known as *Guy Domville*. Alexander offered him royalties of £5 a performance with a ceiling of £2,000, after which the full rights to go to the actor-manager, and James replied: 'I should be obliged to you if you can put the case to me more dazzlingly another way.' It is not known what terms were decided between them.

Leon Edel says of Alexander that, although he was not a man of large imagination, he compensated for this by a kind of furious energy. He surrounded himself with good actors and showed discrimination in his choice of plays. In the winter of 1894 James wrote to his brother that his play would be 'exquisitely mounted, dressed &c. and as well acted as London can act'. Later he wrote asking him to 'unite in family prayer for me on Saturday, January 5 at 8.30,' and to a friend that 'the dew of agony is already on my brow....' On 3 January he wrote: 'I have changed my policy. I recognise that the only way for me to arrive at 10 o'clock with any patience is to *do* something active or at least positive; so I have had the luminous idea of going to see some other play.' And he added: 'I am more or less already under chloroform.'

On 5 January in this rather indecent state of fear he went to the Haymarket to see *An Ideal Husband*. He did not enjoy Wilde's play: he found it crude, clumsy, feeble and vulgar. How could his play, he asked himself, possibly succeed with a public who enjoyed this one.

Meanwhile one of the most brilliant first-night audiences that have ever assembled sat in the stalls of the St James's Theatre. It included Sir Edward Burne-Jones, Sir Frederick

Leighton, G. F. Watts, George du Maurier and John Singer Sargent. Graham Robertson was there, and Mrs Humphry Ward, Edmund Gosse and Thomas Anstey Guthrie (F. Anstey); Elizabeth Robins and Kate and Florence Terry; Bernard Shaw (in the first week of his life as a dramatic critic), H. G. Wells and Arnold Bennett.

The curtain rose on an elaborate and realistic representation of a garden, and in this setting, Leon Edel tells us, 'the actors caught and sustained the romantic mood', while 'the graceful and rhythmic dialogue. . . delighted the audience'. The first act was as well received as the playwright could have wished and at the fall of the curtain the audience, genuinely moved, felt itself in the presence of an exceptional dramatic talent. 'Whatever may have been hoped for from the author of such a first act [Leon Edel writes] was not the act that followed.'

In the second act Guy Domville, a devout and noble churchman, destined in the first act for the ministry, falls at a reckless speed for the rather crude temptations that are placed in his way. He is seen as a swaggering dandy, embroiled in a theatrical intrigue; and on the first night he was required to take part in a scene, afterwards cut, in which two characters, both shamming drunkenness, attempted to make the other drunk. Leon Edel writes: 'James had yielded to the clap-trap of artificial drama, to the *ficelle* structure of Sardou and the other dramatists he had studied with such assiduity at the Théâtre Français. . . .'

The trouble was that in the realm of artificial drama James had none of Sardou's natural talent. One critic wrote, after seeing *The American*: 'We are as anxious as the critics of the newest school to hail the advent on our stage of literary men, but it is on condition that they bring their literature with them.'

In the third act James returned to the scene and to the mood of the first act. But it was by now too late. Coughing and fidgeting in the audience had created a tension which made the work of the nervous, first-night cast impossible. There had been tittering and interruptions in the second act and when in the third Alexander spoke the line, 'I'm the last, my lord, of the Domvilles', a voice from the gallery replied, 'It's a bloody good thing you are.'

When Henry James arrived at the St James's Theatre at the

end of the play no one told him that it had been badly received. The curtain came down at first to applause. Calls were taken and Alexander received his accustomed ovation. It is difficult to understand why a manager of his experience did not at this point ring down the curtain, turn up the lights and thank his stars to have reached the end of this uneasy first night without worse mishap. But in reply to a few calls of 'Author' from the stalls Alexander led Henry James on to the stage and at that moement pandemonium broke loose. In Henry James's words: 'All the forces of civilisation in the house waged a battle of the most gallant, prolonged and sustained applause with the hoots and jeers and catcalls of the roughs (like those of a cage of beasts at some infernal zoo). . . .' And Leon Edel tells us that it seemed like hours that James and Alexander stood on the stage listening to the 'sound of public scorn'.

He [James] stood there thunderstruck. The dark beard framed a half-open mouth, set off the pallor of the cheeks, the shocked stare. . . . Then James, in those seconds that seemed like hours, standing there white and tense, made a deprecatory gesture, a movement of the arms, a shrug of the shoulders. Alexander shifted nervously from one position to another. The novelist turned suddenly and fled, with Alexander close behind him.

On the following day the critics showed a great and almost unanimous desire to sustain and support Henry James. Bernard Shaw, writing one of his first dramatic criticisms, summed up with his usual spontaneous vigour the feelings of the more educated minority.

When some unmannerly playgoer . . . chooses to send a derisive howl from the gallery at such a situation, we are sorrowfully to admit, if you please, that Mr. James is no dramatist, on the general ground that 'the drama's laws the drama's patrons give.' Pray, which of its patrons? the cultivated majority who, like myself and all the ablest of my colleagues, applauded Mr. James on Saturday, or the handful of rowdies who brawled at him? It is the business of the dramatic critic to educate these dunces, not to echo them.

In an analysis of the qualities and faults of *Guy Domville*, he put first among the qualities a rare charm of speech. 'Line after line comes with such a delicate turn and fall that I unhesitatingly challenge any of our popular dramatists to write

a scene in verse with half the beauty of Mr James's prose.'
Second, he said, *Guy Domville* is a story, not a mere situation
hung out on the gallows of a plot, and third, it relies on the
performers not for the brute force of their personalities but
for their finest accomplishments in grace of manner, delicacy of
diction and dignity of style. But of the second act he said that
little of it can be remembered with pleasure and that it had
better 'have been left out'.

James received more letters from sympathisers and well-
wishers than in all his years as a writer, and on subsequent
nights *Guy Domville* was courteously received. At the end of a
run of four weeks James wrote that 'what appears largely to
have enabled *Guy Domville* to go even a month is the fact that
almost everyone who has been to see it at all appears to have
been three or four times.' But in spite of so much genuine
sympathy and praise he wrote to Elizabeth Robins: 'It has
been a great relief to feel that one of the most detestable
incidents of my life has closed.'

With the failure of *Guy Domville* Alexander had to find a
play to take its place. In the summer of 1894 Oscar Wilde had
been considering writing a farcical comedy and he had written
Alexander the following letter.

The real charm of the play, if it is to have a charm, must be in
the dialogue. The plot is slight, but I think, adequate. . . . Well, I
think an amusing thing with lots of fun and wit might be made. If
you think so too, and care to have the refusal of it, do let me know
and send me £150. If when the play is finished, you think it too
slight – not serious enough – of course you can have the £150 back.
I want to go away and write it, and it could be ready in October, as
I have nothing else to do. . . . In the meanwhile, my dear Aleck,
I am so pressed for money that I don't know what to do. Of course
I am extravagant. You have always been a good wise friend to me,
so think what you can do.

In August 1894 Wilde sent Alexander the scenario of a
different play, one that was eventually written up by Frank
Harris as *Mr and Mrs Daventry*, but later in the year he returned
to his first idea and wrote to Alexander:

As you wished to see my somewhat farcical comedy, I send you
the first copy of it. It is called *Lady Lancing* on the cover: but the

real title is *The Importance of Being Earnest*. When you read the play you will see the punning title's meaning. Of course, the play is not suitable to you at all: you are a romantic actor: the people it wants are people like Wyndham or Hawtrey. Also, I would be sorry if you altered the definite artistic line of progress you have always followed at the St. James's. But, of course, read it, and let me know what you think of it. I have very good offers from America for it.

Wilde may have been seriously in doubt as to Alexander's suitability for the play, because after writing these letters he gave it to Charles Wyndham. But with the failure of *Guy Domville*, Alexander was in a hurry to find a play and he asked Wyndham, who was not in any immediate hurry, to let him have it.

Alexander engaged Allan Aynesworth to play Algernon Moncreiffe, Rose Leclercq for Lady Bracknell, Irene Vanbrugh and Evelyn Millard for the two girls, and among the small-part players were Franklin Dyall and Kinsey Peile. In spite of this excellent cast, rehearsals did not at first run smoothly. Wilde interrupted continually and made it impossible for the actors to get through the play. Finally Alexander took him aside and said that they now understood everything he wanted. 'If you'll leave us alone to get on with the rehearsals we shall try our best to give it to you. But if you don't we shall never be ready. So I'll send you a box for the first night and see you again after the performance.' Wilde was at first rather taken aback but, in dramatic mood, he asked Alexander and Aynesworth to dinner for the purpose of confiding to them, 'You are neither of you my favourite actor'. Yet he stayed away from the theatre. On the first performance, 14 February 1895, he spent most of the evening behind the scene standing in the wings. After the play's phenomenal success, he went to see Alexander who asked him what he had thought of it. 'My dear Aleck [he replied] it was charming, quite charming. And do you know, from time to time I was reminded of a play I once wrote myself called *The Importance of Being Earnest*.'

Earlier he had written to Franklin Dyall: 'I don't think I shall take a call tonight. You see, I took one only last month at the Haymarket, and one feels so much like a *German band*.' Today it is well known that the reason Wilde spent his evening behind the scenes and refused to take a call was because he knew that Lord Queensberry intended to create a disturbance. George Alexander, warned of this possibility, had cancelled the seat booked in his name. When Lord Queensberry arrived with his bouquet of carrots and turnips he was prevented from entering the front door of the theatre, and after trying every other door, including the stage door, he finally went away.

In March, two nights before the libel suit, Wilde dined with his wife and Lord Alfred Douglas and the three of them went to a box at the St James's Theatre to watch his play. Lord Alfred Douglas has told us that Constance Wilde was very much agitated and at the end of the evening had tears in her eyes. (She saw him only once again, visiting him in prison after his mother died.) In spite of this Oscar paid a call on George Alexander between the acts in an airy mood.

'I don't think you ought to have come to the theatre at such a time' – Alexander said – 'people will consider it in bad taste.'

'Are you going to accuse everyone in the theatre of bad taste for seeing my play at such a time?' Wilde asked – 'I would consider it in bad taste if they went to anyone else's play.'

'Do be serious.'

'Then you mustn't be funny.'

In April, after Wilde had been arrested and taken to Holloway Goal, Alexander omitted his name from the posters and the programmes of *The Importance of Being Earnest*. Mason enters the defence for him that, aware of Wilde's financial difficulties, he believed he was doing the best thing for the author as well as for himself in thus attempting to suppress his connection with the play. When Wilde was made bankrupt Alexander bought outright and for very little the acting rights of *Lady Windermere's Fan* and *The Importance of Being Earnest*.

He was to meet Wilde, according to Mason once more, but in fact twice more. On 27 December 1898, in a letter to Robert Ross from the Hôtel des Bains, Napoule, Wilde wrote: 'Yesterday I was beside the sea and suddenly George Alexander appeared on a bicycle. He gave me a crooked, sickly smile, and hurried on without stopping. How absurd and mean of him!' Before the publication of this letter Frank Harris had told the story of this meeting, with some embellishments, in his life of

Wilde; Mason, quoting from him, does his best to dispose of it altogether. 'If there were any basis for the story at all, it might be that either Wilde mistook his bicycler or Alexander did not see Wilde. But it may well have been manufactured. Frank Harris was not very scrupulous whether the blow was fair, so long as the blow was dealt.'

However, Hesketh Pearson, writing much later, and with the evidence of the letter to Robert Ross, says that long afterwards George Alexander told Ross that he had been ashamed of his behaviour at Napoule and that, because of it, on seeing Wilde walking in Paris one day, he had got out of his cab to speak to him. Alexander had made a very good bargain in buying the rights of Wilde's two plays and how he generously agreed to send Wilde £20 every month. After Wilde's death he paid royalties to his estate on revivals of the plays, although he need not have done so, and on his death he left the rights to Wilde's son. Thus he made honourable amends for an involuntary failure in friendship.

Following the failure of *Guy Domville* and the withdrawal of *The Importance of Being Earnest* Alexander put on a play by Henry Arthur Jones with the title *The Triumph of the Philistines*.

At the end of 1906 when Alexander was forty-eight, his biographer tells us, his thoughts and ambition were taking a new direction. 'At one time he had it in mind to put some other actor into the St James's Theatre as its protagonist and to confine himself to running it as a business. At another he thought of letting it. His own hopes were beginning to be set on public service.'

In 1907 he stood at the LCC elections as candidate for South St Pancras, representing the Moderate Party, and won the seat. He continued to act eight times a week but he gave great enthusiasm and care to the LCC, serving on many committees and becoming chairman in 1909 of the Parks and Open Spaces Committee. He began also to develop a greater political ambition and would have liked to stand for Westminster. He had difficulty in finding a seat, however, and by the time one seemed in prospect he was known to be suffering from a serious disease. In 1911 he was knighted for his services to the theatre

but by 1912 he was forced to give up his work on the LCC.
He was suffering from diabetes for which at that time there
was no cure. In spite of this he continued for some time to act
and to manage his theatre. When the war came the system of
actor-management, which had been so successful since the Bancroft's early days at the Prince of Wales's Theatre, was no longer
able to meet the demands of the distracted public, who cared
only for musical plays, revues or spy plays that ended in serious
defeat for the Germans. Alexander produced five plays between
the autumn of 1914 and the summer of 1915 and acted in them
all, but all of them lost money. Later with a comedy of Pinero's
called *The Big Drum* and a play called *The Aristocrat* he
brought his reign to a successful end. He died of consumption
in 1918.

Among the plays of note that Alexander produced during
his twenty-seven years in addition to those already mentioned
were *The Prisoner of Zenda* and *Rupert of Hentzau* by Anthony
Hope, *The Witness for the Defence* by his biographer A. E. W.
Mason and *His House in Order* by Sir Arthur Pinero. A play
called *Bella Donna* by the best-selling novelist Robert Hichens
in collaboration with James Fagan deserves to be mentioned
because after *His House in Order* it was the most financially
successful play he ever put on.

Alexander was a very talented if not a great actor. He was
an excellent administrator and an excellent judge of a play.
These qualities combined to make his long period at the St
James's memorable in the history of the theatre.

Sir Johnston Forbes-Robertson
1853-1937

In July 1951 the BBC Third Programme broadcast a programme called 'Actors Speaking of Hamlet', in which many different actors spoke one of the famous speeches from that play. Several of these voices, including those of Johnston Forbes-Robertson and of Herbert Beerbohm Tree, were from the past, whilst others were those of contemporary actors. Forbes-Robertson spoke the advice of the players, and with the disadvantages of a comparitively early recording and of belonging to an age in which the acting conventions were not only very pronounced but very different from those of today, his performance seemed to be surpassed only by that of Sir John Gielgud. He was a very fine actor and a man of exceptional taste and talent. If in the constellation of stars his light shines with less than the illumination of the very brightest, the reasons for this will appear. One is that he was simply less flashy than many of his fellows. A man of intellect and education as well as of great beauty, he was the forerunner of the school of acting of our own day.

Forbes-Robertson was the child of a romantic union. His father saw his mother walking in the street and fell so deeply in love that he wrote to her asking her to marry him. This couple were of the upper middle classes, secure and cultivated, and Johnston Forbes-Robertson's childhood was very different from that of most of the actors who were his contemporaries. His growing pains were of a kind possible only in a sheltered and civilised society, safe from poverty and free from fear.

But the world in which Forbes-Robertson grew up had more

and rarer things to offer than those which result from security, education and leisure. His father was an art critic who for years wrote on the *Sunday Times* under the name of 'Artis Amator' and whose book *Great Painters of Christendom* was a review of artists from Cimabue to Turner. His mother was so gifted as a painter that her son believed, had she been given opportunities to study, she would have made a name for herself. These two belonged to a small world inhabited by many of the most talented people in England. When as a schoolboy their eldest son began to display an interest in acting and presented to them a performance of *Hamlet* in which his sister, Ida, doubled the parts of Ophelia and the grave-digger, the audience included Ford Madox Brown and his wife, Alma-Tadema, Richard Garnett, Dante Gabriel Rossetti and, 'lying on the floor in front of them all, close to "the floats", Swinburne, who disconcerted me somewhat by lowly chanting the lines in his melodious voice in unison with mine.'

On different evenings this child heard Swinburne declaim the whole of Webster's *Vittoria Corombona* (*The White Devil*) and much of *The Duchess of Malfi* and once heard him give a reading of *Atalanta in Calydon*, just before its publication, all in a 'sort of chant'. Once, when he himself had delivered a reading of some scenes from *King Lear*, one of his mother's guests taught him an exercise for the voice. Striking a note on the piano he instructed him not to sing but to speak a line of six or seven words on that note, afterwards repeating it from note to note until he was as high as it was possible for him to speak. Thus even as a child he learned to extend his speaking register and to acquire flexibility and variety of tone, and he tells us he carried on the practice for years, finding it 'of great help, especially in long sustained passages'.

In the houses of his parents' friends the world of painting was made as free to him as that of literature. (When Rossetti painted the picture of *Dante's Dream* in which Mrs William Morris sat as Beatrice, he borrowed the young Johnston Forbes-Robertson to sit for the head of Eros.) And every summer he spent his holidays in France in the company of a celebrated priest named Victor Godfroi who taught him the French language and an appreciation of Gothic architecture.

Thus he grew up saturated with all the arts of the civilised world and with an inherited taste that was developed and refined from birth. One day Rossetti, visiting his father's house, saw some of the boy's work in oil-colour and advised that he should study painting. As a result at the age of sixteen he was sent to 'Heatherley's in Newman Street, to draw from the Antique, to the end that I might compete for a studentship at the Royal Academy.' At Heatherley's he made friends with a young man who was anxious to become a student at the Academy but who failed again and again to pass into it. One day this friend gave him a small book he had written which had just been published. The student's name was Samuel Butler and the book was *Erewhon*. A photograph of Johnston Forbes-Robertson dressed in a suit of armour was taken by Samuel Butler at this time.

Unlike his friend, Forbes-Robertson passed easily into the Royal Academy and while he was there came in contact with Landseer, Millais and Leighton. At the end of the period W. G. Wills, the dramatist (whom Shaw had called 'the resident dramatist' at the Lyceum), having seen him act as a child, came to his parents' house with a proposal that he should take a part in his play, *Mary Queen o' Scots*, then running at the Princesse's Theatre in Oxford Street. 'Though I had a great love of the theatre [Forbes-Robertson wrote later], it was no wish of mine to become an actor, but I was the eldest of a large family, and it was time for me to get out of the nest and make my own living.' With these few casual words Forbes-Robertson dismisses his whole career as a painter, for which he had spent four years in preparation, and describes his entry into the theatre where he was soon to make his name. We may wonder in vain why his parents so easily allowed him to abandon a career in art for which he had proved that he had considerable talent, and why without hesitation they allowed him to join a profession which was so little respected and, except in the case of the very few, so poorly paid. All we know is that the next day this youth found himself reciting to Mrs Rousby, the actress who played Mary Queen of Scots, that he was approved and that within three or four days he made his first appearance on the professional stage. Nor, after this fortuitous introduction to the dramatic art, did he apparently ever consider taking up any other career. His youthful beauty and natural ability

were so considerable, however, that it is not surprising that
Wills, looking for a juvenile, should have thought of him.

Mary Queen o' Scots was not a great success and was soon
withdrawn. The young Forbes-Robertson was immediately
re-engaged, this time by Charles Reade to play in *The Wandering Heir*, the play for which, after meeting her struggling with
a pony cart in a lane, Reade had brought Ellen Terry back to
London. Reade suggested to him that it would be a good thing
if he called and introduced himself to Miss Terry and he made
the journey to Taviton Street where, like so many others, he
was impressed by the straw-coloured matting, the grey-blue of
the Japanese patterns on the hangings and the life-size Venus
de Milo, and where, again like so many others, he fell in love
with the young actress. Later he was to write of this first
meeting: 'Presently the door opened, and in floated a vision of
loveliness! In a blue kimono and with that wonderful golden
hair, she seemed to melt into the surroundings and appeared
almost intangible. . . . I was undergoing a sort of inspection,
but her manner was so gracious that it soon cleared away my
embarrassment.' While Miss Terry wrote of him: 'Everyone
knows how good-looking he is now, but as a boy he was
wonderful – a dreamy, poetic-looking creature in a blue smock,
far more of an artist than an actor – he promised to paint quite
beautifully – and full of aspirations and ideals.' Nevertheless,
Miss Terry did not at this time think much of Forbes-Robertson's
potentialities as an actor and she advised him to give up the
theatre and stick to painting.

He bore a charmed life and his passage to the forefront of
the profession he had chosen was assured. Immediately after
playing in *The Wandering Heir* he was engaged by Charles
Calvert, of the Prince's Theatre, Manchester. In those days Manchester was a considerable artistic centre. Charles Hallé was
conducting his orchestra and Calvert's productions were
celebrated all over the country. Forbes-Robertson writes:

Calvert had been reviving some of Shakespeare's plays with great
intelligence and taste. . . . All to do with the stage was designed by
the best artists of the time, and it is doubtful if ever before Shakespeare had been put upon the stage so correctly, from an archaeological point of view. Macready, Charles Kean and Phelps had paved
the way in a measure, but between their time and Calvert's the

arts had developed in every direction, and many books on costume became available, notably those of Planché, Racinet, and Viollet-le-Duc.

But great as was his good fortune in playing with this company, so suited to develop his own tastes and talents, these years were even more notable for his meeting with Samuel Phelps. The time came when Calvert's stock company was called upon to support the veteran actor in revivals of *A Midsummer Night's Dream* and *Henry IV Part II*. In the latter play Phelps doubled the parts of Henry IV and Justice Shallow and Forbes-Robertson played Prince Hal. During the first rehearsal of the scene between the King and Prince, Phelps suddenly spoke: 'Young man,' he said, 'you know nothing about this part; come to my dressing-room tonight at seven o'clock.' From that day there developed between the old actor and the young a special relationship in which Phelps not merely coached Forbes-Robertson but seldom again played an engagement without him. Later Forbes-Robertson wrote: 'He [Phelps] had been Macready's favourite actor. Macready had played with Mrs Siddons, and she had played with Garrick.' Thus the voice that was heard on the BBC sound programme in 1951 belonged to an actor in the direct line from Garrick.

A few months before Phelps died Forbes-Robertson painted his portrait dressed as Wolsey, the last part he ever played, and this was bought by the members of the Garrick Club where it hangs today.

Since they were always on the look-out for gifted young actors, it was inevitable that sooner or later Johnston Forbes-Robertson should join the Bancrofts at the Prince of Wales's Theatre. This he did in 1878, when he had been three years on the stage, taking over the part of Orloff in *Diplomacy* from Bancroft himself. In 1879 he played again with the Bancrofts' company in *Duty*, an adaptation by James Albery of a play by Sardou, and in *Ours*. He was much impressed by the consideration and courtesy shown the company by this management, particularly in the matter of the payment of salaries. He had so bitterly resented the usual custom by which actors waited in a queue on Saturday morning that on one occasion he had gone without his salary for three weeks rather than submit to it.

In the summer of 1880 Forbes-Robertson met Modjeska, the Polish actress who was regarded, with Duse and Bernhardt, as among the greatest of the nineteenth century. She made her reputation in America and played only for a short time in London, afterwards retiring from the stage and living with her husband in California. Forbes-Robertson first played Romeo to her Juliet at a charity performance in a rectory garden in Cornwall, but later he played it in London at the Court Theatre. Sir George Arthur tells us that she tried a good many leading men but 'there is reason to think that the one who approached most nearly to her ideal was Johnston Forbes-Robertson, her Maurice de Saxe and her Romeo.'

In October 1882 Forbes-Robertson played for the first time with Irving at the Lyceum. He played Claudio in *Much Ado About Nothing* and very much surprised Miss Terry, who ten years before had advised him to give up acting and stick to painting. He was quite exceptional among young actors in the Lyceum company in that he had a constitutional incapacity to 'play a table leg'. Bernard Shaw, speaking of the qualities required of a juvenile under the star system, said: 'His great secret is to keep quiet, look serious, and, above all, not act. To this day you see Mr Lewis Waller and Mr George Alexander struggling, even in the freedom of management, with the habits of the days when they were expected to supply this particular style of article, and to live under the unwritten law: "Be a nonentity, or you will get cast for villains." ' But he added: 'Only for certain attractive individual peculiarities which have enabled Mr Forbes-Robertson to place himself above this law occasionally as a personal privilege, our stage heroes would be as little distinguishable from one another as bricks in a wall.'

As soon as Forbes-Robertson began to get parts in plays that settled down for a run he used the leisure from rehearsals to give time to his first love, painting. He came under the influence of Millais who encouraged him in this work and got him several commissions to paint portraits. Now, at the Lyceum, Henry Irving commissioned him to paint the church scene in *Much Ado About Nothing* where the marriage between Claudio and Hero is suddenly interrupted. This picture, which includes the figures of himself, William Terriss and Evelyn Millard as well

15 *top Lady Windermere's Fan.*
Left to right: Ben Webster, A.
Vane Tempest, Nutcombe Gould,
H. M. Vincent, George Alexander.
St James's Theatre, 1892.

16 *bottom* Alexander as Guy
Domville in the second act of
Guy Domville, the occasion of
Henry James's theatrical disaster.
St James's Theatre, 1895.

17 Alexander and Mrs Patrick
Campbell in *The Second Mrs
Tanqueray*. St James's Theatre,
1893.

Sir Herbert Beerbohm Tree

18   A cartoon of Tree by Max
Beerbohm.

19 Malvolio. Remarking that Tree was 'a richly creative comedian', Max Beerbohm said, 'His Svengali and his Malvolio abide in my mind as two of his especial triumphs.' His Majesty's Theatre, 1901.

20 Fagin in *Oliver Twist*, a stage adaptation by J. Comyns Carr. One of Tree's greatest roles. His Majesty's Theatre, 1905.

21 Tree as Svengali in *Trilby*, the play by Paul Potter adapted from the novel by George du Maurier. This play made a fortune and enabled Tree to build Her Majesty's Theatre. Haymarket Theatre, 1895.

24 Tree as Beethoven in the play of that name adapted by L. N. Parker from the play by René Fauchois. This play was a failure but memorable for Tree's extraordinary transformation for the name part. 1909.

Shylock in *The Merchant of* *:e.* His Majesty's Theatre,

25 *top* Du Maurier as the original Dodor in Tree's production of *Trilby*, with Herbert Ross as Fouzou. Haymarket Theatre, 1895.

26 *bottom* As Raffles in the play of that name with Laurence Irving (the second son of Sir Henry Irving) as Crawshay. Comedy Theatre, 1906.

top : *Diplomacy* : the 1913 production with du Maurier as Henry Beauclerc – the part once played by Squire Bancroft – Gladys Cooper as Dora and Annie Schletter as the Marquise de Rio-Zares. Wyndham's Theatre, 1913.

28 bottom : *The Last of Mrs Cheyney*. Gerald du Maurier as Lord Dilling overhears the conversation between Ronald Squire as Charles, the butler, and Gladys Gray as Lady Joan, during which he recognises Charles as a crook. St. James's Theatre, 1925.

29 Du Maurier as Sir John Marley
in *Interference* by Ronald Pertwee
and Harold Dearden. St James's
Theatre, 1927.

as those of Ellen Terry and Henry Irving, now hangs in the Players' Club in New York.

In November 1883 Forbes-Robertson joined the Bancroft company, by now at the Haymarket, for the third time, and on this occasion remained with them for nearly two years until their retirement in 1885. Then he crossed the Atlantic, for the first of many times, to become Mary Anderson's leading man for an extensive tour of America. Mary Anderson was so great a beauty that when she played at the Lyceum audiences were attracted merely to see her much-famed face. She was ranked by Sir George Arthur with Mrs Rousby – with whom Forbes-Robertson had played his first part in *Mary Queen o' Scots* – Adelaide Neilson, Mrs Langtry and Gladys Cooper, as among the greatest beauties of the stage. The impressionable Forbes-Robertson once more fell deeply in love. At first this feeling seems to have been returned and the two became engaged; but on her return to England Miss Anderson met a Mr de Navarro, a rich man who like herself was a Roman Catholic, and she broke her engagement to marry him. According to the account of his niece, Beatrice, Forbes-Robertson felt deeply unhappy.

He seems to have had no great desire to become an actor-manager: on his return to England he drifted from one theatre to another for a while, and then joined John Hare with whom he remained for six years. During this time he was several times released, once to go again to New York and twice to join Irving at the Lyceum. The first of his Lyceum engagements was to play Buckingham in *Henry VIII*, the second, to play Launcelot in Comyns Carr's *King Arthur*. Then in 1895, when he was 38, he began to feel that it was necessary to his career for him to go into management for himself. He says:

I would gladly have remained an actor pure and simple, to be called off the ranks, so to speak, by anyone who wished to engage me. For over twenty-one years I had great good fortune in not only being in continual engagement, but in having been associated with the best managements. Calvert, Hollingshead, Neville, the Bancrofts, Miss Mary Anderson, Clayton, Hare and Irving. I had acted with all the leading people of that time and, though at periods being very hard worked, I had comparatively no anxieties. The very speculative and gambling nature of theatrical management was distasteful to me, and I knew that my own personal efforts as

E

an actor would be considerably handicapped by all the extra labour and anxiety which management entails. On the other hand, several actors, younger than I, had taken up management very much earlier in their careers, and there was nothing for it but to take a theatre if I was to maintain my place. Though it is true that an ideal theatre would be that in which the manager did not act, the fact remains that all the ambitious work, all the higher standards of the Drama have been maintained by the much-abused actor-manager from the days of Shakespeare down to our own time.

In the autumn of 1895 Irving left London for a long tour of America and Forbes-Robertson took over the Lyceum during his absence. He engaged Mrs Patrick Campbell as his leading lady and opened with *Romeo and Juliet*. Alan Dent says: 'The noble actor was by this time "getting on" and he really ought to have given the world his Hamlet, his masterpiece, before he was forty-four years of age [1897]. There is implanted in the family [Forbes-Robertson's family] a strong conviction that he would have done so in the first Lyceum season, beginning 1895, if Mrs Campbell had not prevailed on him to play Romeo instead.'

During this first season in management Forbes-Robertson also put on a play by Henry Arthur Jones called *Michael and His Lost Angels* – chiefly remembered for the quarrels between the author and Mrs Patrick Campbell, who resigned her part with the maximum possible sensation shortly before the first night, an adaptation of François Coppée's *Pour La Couronne*; Louis N. Parker's adaptation of Sudermann's *Heimat* under the name of *Magda*, and *The School for Scandal*. It was not an immensely successful season; both Henry Arthur Jones's play and *Magda* – later to be one of Mrs Patrick Campbell's most famous roles – had to be quickly replaced because business was bad. His production of *Romeo and Juliet* was much admired, although Bernard Shaw said of him that 'his sense of colour is essentially and Britannically an imaginative and moral one: that is, he associates low tones ("quiet colours" they call them in Marshall & Snellgrove's) with dignity and decency, and white linen with cleanliness and respectability.' But he compared the results with a recent production of Augustin Daly's and said: 'Mr Daly's scene-painters copied bad work, and Mr

Forbes-Robertson's have copied good. That makes all the difference.'

Forbes-Robertson's performance seems generally to have been regarded as in rather 'low tone'. There is at least a suggestion that the reason for this lay not with his imaginative and moral sense but with the temperament of his leading lady. He says of his opening production as an actor-manager only this: 'The first performance was given under trying circumstances, for Mrs Campbell was very ill and in great pain, Coghlan was paralysed with nervousness at his reappearance in London after many years of absence, and Nutcombe Gould, who played the Friar, had one arm in a sling! . . . I remember my own performance was tame, lacking in fire and the buoyance of youth.' Mrs Patrick Campbell's biographer comments on this: 'Our Stella, being "very ill and in great pain" managed to keep this fact between herself and her new actor-manager, her Romeo. It emerges from none of the astonishingly diverse critical notices.'

Probably the greatest success of the season was *The School for Scandal*, of which Bernard Shaw wrote: 'Mr Forbes-Robertson is an excellent Joseph Surface. He gets at the centre of the part by catching its heartlessness and insincerity, from which his good looks acquire a subtle ghastliness, his grace a taint of artifice, and all the pictorial qualities which make him so admirable as a saint or medieval hero an ironical play which has the most delicate hypocritical effect.'

In July 1897, when Irving was preparing for his second tour to America, Forbes-Robertson had neither the money nor apparently a great inclination to take the theatre again. More important still, he had no play. He was about to abandon the idea of a second season altogether when Horatio Bottomley offered to back him. At the same time Irving suggested a play, offering to lend him the scenery and properties for *Hamlet*.

At his first performance of *Hamlet* at the Lyceum Forbes-Robertson was everywhere acclaimed the greatest Hamlet of his day. He took over that night the mantle from Henry Irving and wore it until he passed it in turn to Sir John Gielgud. The critics were unanimous in their praise and dozens of accounts testify to the particular felicities of this Hamlet whose voice was as beautiful as his face. Once more Bernard Shaw's account

F*

is the most illuminating. Having remarked that at this performance the story of the play was perfectly intelligible and
quite at times took the attention of the audience off the
principal actor, he went on: 'What is the Lyceum coming to?
Is it for this that Sir Henry Irving has invented a whole series
of original romantic dramas, and given the credit of them without a murmur to the immortal bard?...He no sooner turns
his back for a moment on London than Mr Forbes-Robertson
competes with him on the boards of his own theatre by actually
playing off against him the authentic Swan of Avon.' He says
then that Forbes-Robertson is essentially a classical actor, the
only one, with the exception of George Alexander, established
in London management, 'What I mean by classical is that he
can present a dramatic hero whose passions are those which
have produced the philosophy, the poetry, the art, and the
stagecraft of the world, and not merely those which have
produced its weddings, coroners' inquests and executions.'

In the following passage Shaw explains the importance of
Forbes-Robertson's contribution to the theatre. Carrying on the
tradition of the best Shakespearian acting from Phelps, he can
also be seen to have been a forerunner of the greatest actors of
our own day.

Mr Forbes-Robertson's own performance has a continuous
charm, interest, and variety which are the result not only of his
well-known grace and accomplishment as an actor, but of a genuine
delight—the rarest thing on our stage—in Shakespeare's art, and a
natural familiarity with the plane of his imagination. He does not
superstitiously worship William: he enjoys him and understands
his methods of expression. Instead of cutting every line that can
possibly be spared, he retains every gem, in his own part or anyone
else's, that he can make time for in a spiritedly brisk performance
lasting three hours and a half with very short intervals. He does
not utter half a line; then stop to act; then go on with another half
line; and then stop to act again, with the clock running away with
Shakespeare's chances all the time. He plays as Shakespeare should
be played, on the line and to the line, with the utterance and acting
simultaneous, inseparable and in fact identical. Not for a moment
is he solemnly conscious of Shakespeare's reputation or of Hamlet's
momentousness in literary history: on the contrary, he delivers
us from all these boredoms instead of heaping them on us. . . . How

completely Mr Forbes-Robertson has bowled them all out by being clever enough to be simple.

On 4 September Ellen Terry wrote to Bernard Shaw:

I only saw the last two scenes of the last act of Hamlet. . . . I could not gather much . . . about the acting. I went in the dark and heard whisperings that the people liked Johnston, and didn't like anything else, and I saw a very good Norse-like picture of Hamlet's death, heard Johnston's voice, and saw his poor dear face, worn to tatters, but now and again very beautiful.

And on 7 September she wrote again: 'I came back early from the country and (passing his door) went in and pulled the new Hamlet out of bed. Poor fellow. Hamlet's mother and young sisters and I cheered him up a bit. He looks sadly old for a young man. His poor long face.'

These pitying words, written about someone who had so recently reached the height of every great actor's ambition, are difficult to understand. But Bernard Shaw would have required no explanation of them, because it was widely known that Johnston Forbes-Robertson, who had once loved Ellen Terry, was now in thrall to a fury.

Mrs Patrick Campbell was one of the finest actresses of her time, and her natural beauty of face and figure were much enhanced by a physical coordination which gave every movement she made on the stage significance as well as grace. Her speaking voice was one of her natural charms and she had intelligence and wit. She was entrancingly attractive but she may fairly be said to have been possessed of a devil. In the long run she received even less mercy from this fiend than she felt for other people, and the day would come when, no manager daring to allow her inside a theatre, she 'toured and toured with unrewarding parts in unremarkable plays, a respected living legend but none the less an actress-mis-manageress', and later still when she would live out her life in idleness and poverty. But when she was young and at the height of her powers she ruthlessly provoked those who, like Alexander, were not under her spell, and those who loved her she savaged.

She rewarded the loves of Forbes-Robertson and (later) the young Gerald du Maurier by systematic torture. She outraged those who played with her because she was not serious in the theatre: when she was in a bad mood she would turn her back on the audience and stand pulling faces at her fellow actors. When Ellen Terry came to see her play Ophelia, she changed from a dark wig to a fair in the middle of the performance because she wished to know which Miss Terry thought suited her better.[1] During the rehearsals for *Hamlet*, Ian Forbes-Robertson, who was stage manager, said to her: 'You know Mrs Campbell, you are killing my brother.'

Forbes-Robertson was of an intense, passionate and sensitive nature. His grand-daughter says, speaking of Stella Campbell: He reacted to her flippancies with violence and suffering.' In the end he became physically ill and was forced to leave the stage and go abroad to recover his health. But this was not for four years and during this time she remained his leading lady.

Hamlet was played every night for a record run of over 100 performances. Forbes-Robertson found this exhausting. No actor, he said, should play any classic role more than three or four times a week. Then in February 1898 he took his company on tour in Germany and Holland, playing *Hamlet*, *Macbeth* and (for Mrs Campbell) *The Second Mrs Tanqueray* in Berlin, Hanover, Hamburg and Amsterdam.

Mrs Patrick Campbell's presence in his company influenced his choice of plays. For her sake, and rather against his own judgment, on his return to London he put on Maeterlinck's play *Pelleas and Melisande*. Forbes-Robertson played Golaud and cast Martin Harvey as Pelleas. 'Why do you want to make such a damned fool of Forbes?' Ian Forbes-Robertson asked her at the rehearsals of this play. Today *Pelleas and Melisande* is not often performed except as Debussy's opera but it has the fragile distinction of a myth and a place in the accumulation of the world's literature. Forbes-Robertson's Macbeth to Mrs Campbell's Lady Macbeth was not regarded as a great success for either.

In 1899, after a disastrous failure in joint management with a play called *The Moonlight Blossom*, by C. B. Fernald, the two parted and Forbes-Robertson, advised by his doctor and his friends to take a long rest, went abroad. When towards the end

---

[1] Mrs Patrick Campbell was not generally very much admired as Ophelia and in her book she says: 'The real truth was that Miss Terry had given such a lovely Ophelia to the world – still fresh in everyone's memory – that there was no room for mine'.

of this holiday Ian Forbes-Robertson began to engage a company for his brother to return to, he sent him a list of possible leading ladies. On the list was the name of a young American actress, Gertrude Elliott, the sister of the more famous Maxine.

Miss Elliott was not Forbes-Robertson's first choice because he wanted a leading lady with experience of playing Shakespeare and he sent a different name to his brother. Three days later he telegraphed: 'If not too late engage Miss Elliott.' Leon Quartermain was also engaged for this tour and two new productions were given – *The Devil's Disciple* and *Carrots* – an English version by Alfred Sutro of the play by Jules Renard – in which the new leading lady played the persecuted boy.

On 8 November we find Bernard Shaw writing to tell Ellen Terry: 'News this morning that the incontinent youth Johnston Forbes-Robertson is going to be led to the altar by his leading lady, Miss Gertrude Elliott. I foresaw it, and wanted to put a clause in the contract against it. However, he might do worse. She is a nice American woman and will mend his extensively broken heart.'[1] In fact this was in Forbes-Robertson's own words 'the prelude of nothing less to me than a supremely happy life.' The Forbes-Robertsons had four daughters, all of whom inherited some of their father's talent, and one of whom, Jean, became famous in his profession.

As an actor Johnston Forbes-Robertson scarcely had a failure in any part he played: he was admired by everyone from the ordinary play-going public to the most exacting of the critics. We find Bernard Shaw writing: 'Forbes-Robertson, acting stupdendously well ... while Max Beerbohm, speaking of his performance in *The High Bid*, said: 'The words could not have been more perfectly uttered than they were by Mr Forbes-Robertson. We realised at once to whom *he* beautifully belongs. It is to Mr Henry James.' No words could be higher praise from this critic. Of his performance in *Hamlet* to which he owes his place in history, Hesketh Pearson tells us in the calm of retrospect:

No literary criticism of Hamlet was worth twopence by the side of Forbes-Robertson's dramatic explanation of him. The whole thing was final in its exquisite simplicity. . . . Leaving entirely on

---

[2] Forbes-Robertson was now 43, his bride some 20 years younger.

one side the actor's extraordinary physical grace and the organ-music of his marvellous voice, he was the only artist of his time – I dare guess of any time – who was Hamlet in gesture and speech. He lived in the period and spoke its language. . . . Forbes-Robertson's Hamlet was the only Shakespearean performance one could see twenty times (and twice in one day) yet wish to go on seeing it twenty times twenty.

While speaking of Tree's Hamlet, Desmond MacCarthy said: 'We much preferred the fastidious, scholarly, airy-gallant Hamlet of Forbes-Robertson.'

As a manager Forbes-Robertson's name was never connected with a particular London theatre in the way Irving's was with the Lyceum and Alexander's with the St James's. He spent a very great deal of his time on tour, some of it in the English provinces, even more in America and Canada, and in over twenty years he played only four seasons in London. He was often away for a year or more at a time and he was as well known in New York as in London, in Winnipeg, Montreal, Toronto, Washington, Chicago, Philadelphia as in Liverpool or Manchester. 'We visited [he said of the American tour of 1903] all the leading cities in the east, to the south as far as Rich-mond . . . and westwards to the restless and energetic city of Chicago.' Owing to the American custom of morning per-formances he was sometimes forced to play Hamlet nine times a week and during the course of his visits he watched many of the cities of North Americas change from one night stands to places where his company could perform for a week. When he planned his farewell tour to all the towns where he was known, he found that it would take four years to perform it.

His productions were noted, as might be expected, for their scholarship and taste. His chief Shakespearian productions apart from *Hamlet* were of *Romeo and Juliet*, *Macbeth* and *Othello*. In none of these roles was he transcendent, the temp-erament of the classical actor being less suited to these parts.

In the discovery and production of new plays, he seems to have had neither better nor worse judgment than that of the other actor-managers and his appreciation was neither so fine nor so literary as to bring about a division between his tastes and those of the public he had to please. He chose his plays, as every manager must, to suit this public, but he chose them, too, as every actor must, to suit himself. He had no difficulty in reconciling the two, nor was he lacking in a straightforward business sense. Among the plays to which he gave their first performance the only ones of interest today are *The Devil's Disciple, Caesar and Cleopatra, The High Bid*, a dramatised version of *The Light that Failed* – a play that caused Max Beerbohm to ask himself whether perhaps Rudyard Kipling was the pseudonym of a woman – and a curious play, forgotten today but with which, after *Hamlet*, his name was most often associated, called *The Passing of the Third Floor Back*.

Caesar and Cleopatra was written for Forbes-Robertson but Bernard Shaw could not persuade him to produce it for several years. In 1899 he wrote to Ellen Terry: 'Forbes-Robertson has given up Caesar. "Can't run the risk of such a heavy production." Is going on tour next Sept. instead of opening a new theatre – wants the last act of *The Devil's Disciple* altered into an English victory. I have cut him off without a shilling.' When Forbes-Robertson finally produced it, he did so at the Amsterdam Theatre, New York, and then took it on tour in America and Canada. It is an interesting fact that after being very well received in all these places, it failed at a subsequent production in London. Forbes-Robertson says that in some places it was said that the reason it succeeded in New York and failed in London was that the New York audiences were less sophisticated – a view, he adds, that was highly amusing to those who knew America's theatre-going public. That this amusement was justified seems to be proved by the fact that *Caesar and Cleopatra* had far more success in London when he played it again at Drury Lane in 1913.

Caesar was, after Hamlet, Forbes-Robertson's greatest role. Hesketh Pearson tells us: 'There has been nothing to compare with it on the stage of my time: a great classical actor interpreting to perfection a self-inspired classical part. . . . There was not a movement or an inflection in his Caesar that could have been bettered.'

The High Bid was written by Henry James originally for Ellen Terry, but when it became clear that she would never put it on the novelist re-wrote it as a short story and called it *Covering End*. Forbes-Robertson, reading this story, was struck by how admirably it might suit the stage. He wrote to James asking if he would be willing to have it turned into a play and James sent him *The High Bid*.[3] Forbes-Robertson gave the play some performances in the provinces but he did not at the time take it to London. He opened instead at the St James's Theatre in Jerome K. Jerome's play *The Passing of the Third Floor Back*. The story of this play is of a lodger in a boarding house in Bloomsbury who so influences the minds of his fellow-lodgers that they are translated to a higher plane of thought and feeling and where they find peace, love and contentment come to them. *The Passing of the Third Floor Back* was held by some to be blasphemous, by others to be merely puerile, but it was one of the greatest successes of its time and, after *Hamlet*, made more money for Forbes-Robertson than any other play. After rebuking the actor-manager for not bringing *The High Bid* into London, Max Beerbohm wrote:

Appparently in doubt whether Mr. James be good enough for the metropolis, he gives us Mr. Jerome Klapka Jerome. This tenth-rate writer has been, for many years, prolific of his tenth-rate stuff. But I do not recall, in such stuff of his as I have happened to sample, anything quite so vilely stupid as 'The Passing of the Third Floor Back.' I do not for a moment suppose that Mr. Forbes-Robertson likes it one whit more than I do. And I wish his pusillanimity in prostituting his great gifts to it were going to be duly punished. The most depressing aspect of the whole matter is that the play is so evidently a great success.

But Max Beerbohm was wrong in thinking Forbes-Robertson prostituted his gifts. On the contrary, when Forbes-Robertson read the play he was at first dismayed because he felt that in the ordinary sense it was no play at all. He says, however, that he gradually became deeply impressed by the elevating character of the theme. He discussed the matter with his wife and they both agreed that although some people might like this play very much these would not be enough to make it profit-

[3] On 27 March 1908 when Forbes-Robertson performed *The High Bid* for the first time at Edinburgh he received a telegram from Ellen: 'You have my play!' Forbes-Robertson writes: 'We then discovered that she did not consider she had parted with her acting rights when agreeing to its being published in story form. It was a most unfortunate misunderstanding, soon, however, cleared up, but embarrassing for me at the time'.

able: it was unlikely to draw. Yet in spite of this they decided that they must produce it. 'The long and short of it was, we were both in love with the high motive of the play, and decided to produce it solely on that score. As time proved, we were well rewarded for our enthusiasm.' They were rewarded in England and all over America and Scotland. *The Passing of the Third Floor Back* turned out to be one of those plays that could be revived again and again and used as a stop-gap when some other play failed.

In June 1913 Johnston Forbes-Robertson received a knighthood. In the same year, although not quite sixty, he started on his long farewell tour of England, Scotland, Canada and America. After playing three months at the Theatre Royal Drury Lane, three months in New York, a month in Chicago and visiting Indianapolis, St Louis, Kansas City, Denver, Salt Lake City, Los Angeles, and San Francisco, he burned all his scenery except that of four plays because from now on he would play in no town long enough to need more. In Portland, Tacoma, Seattle, Victoria, Calgary, Edmonton and Winnipeg he found himself in the midst of preparations for war but he continued on his nomadic way, playing in the last year of his tour only one-night stands.

Here are the words with which this flawless actor, who entered the theatre in response to an invitation and who, almost alone in the ranks of leading actors, never had to struggle for place or admiration, summed up his career:

I stripped myself of Hamlet's garb with no sort of regret, but rather with a great sense of relief, for not only was it my last appearance in a part which cost me a vast amount of mental and physical strain, but the last of theatrical management, the gambling nature of which had always been abhorrent to me. On looking back, it seems to me that I was far more nervous on the last performance of *Hamlet* than on the first. It is said that nervousness is a necessary attribute for the actor, and that he who does not suffer from it is rarely of much account in his art. It may be so, but all I can say is that as far as I personally am concerned, it has been nought but a shackling handicap. Never at any time have I gone on the stage without longing for the moment when the curtain would come down on the last act. Rarely, very rarely have I enjoyed myself in acting. This cannot be the proper mental attitude for an actor, and

I am persuaded, as I look back on my career, that I was not temp-
eramentally suited to my calling.

He lived for more than twenty years, until 1937, happy in
retirement.

Sir Herbert Beerbohm Tree
1853-1917

Sir Herbert Beerbohm Tree succeeded Sir Henry Irving as leader of the theatre. A natural leader of men as well as a great actor, he was born to this role and he revelled in it. He had the grand flamboyant manner and, unlike Irving who was pontifical and awe-inspiring, an irresistible charm. On his death his half-brother, Max Beerbohm, who had grown to dislike biographies of actors, decided against this form of memorial and, saying that Tree was 'many-sided, impressing different people in different ways', he collected together instead a book of short pieces by those who knew him best under the title *Herbert Beerbohm Tree*. Any doubts one might entertain as to the quality of this man are here set at rest by the giftedness of those who testify to it.

He was indeed 'many-sided' and it is possible for his daughter, Viola, to tell us convincingly that he was 'absolutely natural and unaffected' when it is clear from other people's accounts that he exaggerated certain qualities – an absent-mindedness, a whimsical vagueness – and put them to the service of his wit, his privacy and his need to cajole and persuade. But he was in a large way unaffected. Blithely romantic at a time when romanticism was becoming old-fashioned, he carried this off by the size of his undertakings and his own personality: friendly and sensitive, he was, nevertheless, completely self-absorbed. Desmond MacCarthy spoke of his 'restless, dream-glazed eyes which looked at objects in a steady, imperceptive way as though staring at his own thoughts, and that bar above them, which it is said, tends to lift its possessor an inch or two above the solid ground.'

Viola Tree inherited much of her father's nature and she succeeds probably best of anyone in the difficult and delicate task of creating on paper a unique, lively and credible human being. She tells us that Tree 'bore no resemblance to fathers as a race'. He was 'a never-failing excitement, a surprise, an event'. She remembers him best leaning on something, 'always with his hat on and wearing a big, flamboyant coat and carrying some very tall walking stick'. He never entered a room or the garden without called 'Viola!' or 'Children!' which had, she said, the effect of a flourish of trumpets.

He was very dominating, 'almost domineering', 'even to the point of casting out fear'. Thus, when she was rehearsing *The Tempest*:

As his prospective Ariel . . . I had to try the wires . . . and was timidly discussing with the professional on which foot to take off. The wire was, I remember, uncomfortably hooked into my strait waistcoat when he walked on to the stage. 'I always know about these things, dear; don't argue: fly!' and he gave the order to the mechanic up above to let go. Without a murmur I flew, my feet dangling high above his head, and tingling like telegraph wires at the sudden vibrations of his voice. 'Very good, dear; now sing!'

But although he was so dominating, he always thanked his children for being with him. 'So lovely, dear, your being with me.'

Tree was known to be very diffident about his looks and when he went to sit for his portrait to Sargent, who was 'terribly shy and modest about his work', his daughter feared that left to themselves they would never start. So the moment Tree stepped on the dais she called out: 'Look towards the window Daddy.'

He did so. Mr. Sargent became covered with confusion. 'Don't strain, don't strain; you will never be able to keep that pose'. My father seemed surprised and answered: 'No, no, it's quite natural.' This defiant turn of head and illuminated look was normal to him, before whose mind's-eye processions of popes, jugglers and sinister servants holding peacocks in the leash passed continuously to the accompaniment of music, sad, strange or grotesque.

And in a further passage, she says:

I think I shall always remember the last act of *Richard II* as my

best time with him, because in it we did not seem to be on the
stage – we were showing what we really felt about things: that
there was an audience looking on didn't seem to matter. I played
the Queen – very badly, except for the one scene, in which I became myself. I had to wait for his coming (Act V, Scene 1. A Street)
with Aumerle:

> The Queen: This way the King will come; this is the way
> To Julius Ceasar's ill-errected tower—

After this I looked instinctively to see my father come out, very
simply and rather tired, dressed in black, and each time it seemed
as if he were surprised to see me standing there, and as if we were
really to say good-bye to each other for the first and last time. Then
I fell on his neck, and said my speech sobbing, because at that
moment I was not Richard's Queen but my father's daughter – all
alone on the great isolation of the stage, for Aumerle and the super
halberdiers had vanished like shadows to the dark corners. He never
could begin his speech at once – he was so worried by my tears, as
I looked at him through blinded eyes. By and by I put my head
down on his shoulder so that he might begin – then only his voice
came loud and ringing like a clarion:

> Join not with grief, fair woman do not so,
> To make my end too sudden. . . .

Today shame would intervene between us and such large, spontaneous expressions, but in the Trees they rose unrestrainedly
to the surface.

There are many references to Tree's imaginative self-absorp-
tion. Bernard Shaw said that when his feelings were engaged
he was human and shrewd and tenacious but that 'you really
could not lodge an indifferent fact in his mind'. This quality, he
said, was enormously valuable to Tree as an actor because he
avoided staleness by always hearing the other performers' lines
as though for the first time. At a certain point in *Pygmalion*
Mrs Patrick Campbell had to throw a pair of slippers in Tree's
face; and at rehearsal Shaw took great trouble to provide Mrs
Campbell with a very soft pair, because being very dexterous
she was a dead shot. Nevertheless, when the scene was reached
the effect was appalling. Tree had totally forgotten that there
was any such incident in the play; 'and it seemed to him that
Mrs Campbell, suddenly giving away to an impulse of diabolical
wrath and hatred, had committed an unprovoked and brutal

assault on him. The physical impact was nothing; but the wound to his feelings was terrible.'

Tree was gradually reassured by Mrs Campbell and by the entire personnel of the theatre crowding solicitiously round him 'explaining that the incident was part of the play, and even exhibiting the prompt book to prove their words'. But, Shaw wrote, since it was clear Tree would be just as surprised and upset every time this happened, Mrs Campbell took care never to hit him again, and 'the incident was consequently one of the least convincing in the performance'.

Johnston Forbes-Robertson tells us that once in the street outside the theatre stage-door Tree was describing to Edward Sass, a fellow actor, how in his performance of the death of King John, he swept the crown from his head: 'Suiting the action to the word he swept off his hat, then, pointing to it lying in the gutter, and while Sass was spellbound by this unusual proceeding on the part of a distinguished actor in the public street, he asked: "Whose hat is that?" '

These incidents go near to an impression of the aprocryphal or of a great actor play-acting. This occurs again and again in anecdotes about Tree because it was absolutely natural to him to extend reality into the realm of make-believe. Discussing his equipment as an actor, Desmond MacCarthy speaks in a brilliantly explanatory phrase of his 'comprehension of the shifting connection between the heightened pose and the genuine feeling underneath'. An unfortunate result of this smudging of the boundary between the real and the fantastic is that Tree has been over-quoted. It is the duty of all who record the sayings and doings of public men to compensate by rigorous selection for the loss of the powerful personality, the exhilarating charm, behind which in life, as by sleight of hand, the exuberant failures slipped away; but it is a duty too seldom observed. It should have been particularly binding on those who wrote about Tree because of a characteristic Edmund Gosse has described in the following passage:

He was whimsical by nature and his wit was an offshoot of his whim. He tossed his arrows up into the air and sometimes they hit the bull's-eye miraculously; sometimes they did not. I have heard him say things that were deliciously apropos, and with a rapidity of mind that was exhilarating; but I have also heard him murmur things that were almost fatuous; and he seemed to lack personal criticism in this respect. . . . There was always debate behind his back whether Herbert Tree was 'clever' or merely silly, the truth being that he could be both.

Gosse adds, however, that if a quip of his was accepted Tree was pleased, if scornfully rejected 'not less pleased'. His object was 'never to instruct but to stimulate interest'. But the quality which above all made Tree irresistable is described in the following incident: Max Beerbohm tells us that once he was standing on the doorstep of his mother's house with another man when Herbert Tree arrived in a taxi. 'How are you, Mr Tree?' Beerbohm's friend asked. 'I?' said Herbert, shaking the proffered hand and gazing around him. 'I? Oh, I'm radiant.' Later Max's friend remarked to him that from any other man the epithet applied to himself would have seemed absurd, but that Tree's use of it was right and proper. 'He looked radiant, it was obvious that he felt radiant, and he told the simple truth in saying that he *was* radiant.'

It is tempting to speculate on the mature relationship of the two gifted brothers – the exuberant, romantic, popular actor who inevitably produced a broad if 'radiant' impression, and the flawless, perfected Max. Johnston Forbes-Robertson tells us that Tree once said to him: 'There is only one thing I have against Max, it is born in on me that in after years I shall come to be remembered only as Max's brother.' And Max himself encourages speculation, without doing anything to satisfy it, in the following passage:

I am afraid that as the years went by, and the gap between our ages was accordingly contracted, each of us found himself even more shy in presence of the other than he was wont to be with people at large. An old friend of Herbert's once said to him and me, in the course of a dinner in the 'Dome' of His Majesty's: 'You two, when you're together, always seem to be in an attitude of armed neutrality.' I suggested to Herbert that 'terrified love' would be a truer description.

Julius Beerbohm came to London in 1830 at the age of twenty and became a corn merchant. He was a German whose mother was of Slavonic descent and he married an Englishwoman,

Constantia Draper. This couple had three sons, Ernest, Herbert and Julius, and, when Constantia died at under the age of thirty, Julius married her sister Eliza and produced four more children as closely related to the first family as, except for full brothers, it is possible to be. Three of these children were girls and the fourth was Henry Maximilian Beerbohm – the incomparable Max. Nowhere in the history of either the Beerbohm or the Draper families is there anyone to account for the fact that both sisters bore Julius a son of such exceptional talent.

Herbert Draper Beerbohm was born in 1852 and educated partly at schools in England and partly at a school at Schnepfeuthal in Thuringia, where the discipline was of the ruthless cruelty known to us through accounts of German schools at the time. This experience has been held responsible for Herbert Beerbohm growing up to believe that all education was useless and that 'As humour is above wit, so is intelligence above intellect and instinct above knowledge.' But this kind of thought is very common among talented people to whom it is naturally attractive.

Julius Beerbohm became well-established as a corn merchant and, as they grew up, put each of his sons into his own business. None wished to remain there. Ernest, the eldest, departed to become a sheep farmer in Cape Colony where he married a coloured woman, known in his family as a 'brunette', and Julius, the youngest, also went abroad to Patagonia, about which he later wrote a book. Only when his second son announced his wish to become an actor did Julius draw the line. The life of an actor, he said, was all very well if one reached the top of the tree – a remark which is said to have suggested to his son the name he was later to take – but a disreputable and miserable business for everyone else. Herbert, therefore, alone among his sons, remained in his office for eight years, until he was twenty-five.

During his time, like so many of his contemporaries, he taught himself the rudiments of the art of acting in amateur dramatic companies.[1] As can be seen from his photographs he had strange looks, not obviously suited to his chosen profession. He was over six foot tall, his hair was bright red and his

[1] In an amateur society called the 'Philothespians' Tree met two other young city clerks – George Alexander and Lewis Waller.

eyes very blue with pale lashes. He was a natural mimic and he early became known for his imitations of leading actors of the day. For eight years he exhausted himself and his salary travelling about to rehearse and perform in plays, living, as his half-brother described it, in a 'whirl of amateur theatricals'. By February 1878, when he made his first professional performance in a touring company at Folkestone, he had already made some name for himself, and his father reluctantly gave his consent to it. From this time onwards he was always in work, sometimes in London, often on tour, but for several years he made no particular mark. His biographer, Hesketh Pearson writes: 'The oddity of Tree's personality did not appeal to everyone, and in spite of his occasional successes in London no one would have prophesied for him a brilliant future. The managers preferred the type of actor whose appearance and personality attracted women, such as H. B. Conway, who became a *jeune premier* at the Lyceum under Irving and an idol of female playgoers.' And he quotes the lessee of the Vauderville Theatre writing to his acting-manager as follows: 'And now, my dear Smaile, please understand me, I will give Tree £15 a week – not a penny more. H. B. Conway can have £25, as I think he will draw it, but £15 is every shilling as much as Tree is, or ever will be, worth.'

In 1881, when he was twenty-nine, Herbert Tree met Miss Maud Holt, a girl of eighteen who was studying and teaching Latin, Greek and mathematics at Queen's College, Harley Street and intending to go on to Girton. Miss Holt was also very much interested in amateur dramatics and had played Ophelia and Beatrice with amateur companies. A year later Tree asked her to be his wife. The course of this love affair, although it was to last all Tree's life, was not entirely smooth. A number of the letters he wrote her during the course of their engagement survive and have been quoted very fully in Hesketh Pearson's biography. From these it appears that Maud Holt was a strong-willed young lady and one who was inclined to disapprove of the ways of the members of the profession she wished to join. Tree wrote a spontaneous and natural prose and his replies to her strictures are not spoiled, as the letter of his contemporaries so often are, by pompous phraseology. His letters seem tender, solicitous and straightforward.

When he offended his fiancée by giving a scarf to Myra Home (who married Pinero) on her birthday, he wrote to her:

Oh, pray don't think seriously what you spoke hastily, dearest – Only it is so difficult to act strictly according to the cruel letter of what is considered the right thing to do. I assure you most solemnly that I have not broken through the spirit of what is right in doing what I have done – Indeed my only reproach is that I should make you unhappy.

And he tells her that he will pass her house that night after the theatre at about a quarter past eleven. 'If you would see me for only a minute, dear, I should be much happier.'

When Miss Holt spoke of the rumours she had heard about his life before he had met her, he begged her not to be too much influenced by narrow-minded advisers.

I was foolish – perhaps weak – but not vicious or dishonourable. – I gave you to understand, when I first asked you to care for me, that my past life had not been entirely unworldly. I repented what I had done, and you forgave me. I have endeavoured to make every reparation for the error committed before I knew you, and I have been true and loyal to you. – There was never at any time the slightest claim upon me, and I have recently taken steps to remove even the possibility of a shadow in the future. Can I do more? Have I hitherto been impatient of your reproaches, and the attacks of your friends? – To whom do you owe your allegiance – to them or to me? It is for you now to say – I do not care to enter into competition with them – nor will I allow you to despise me, as you would grow to despise me, did not I demand your entire trust, and a love which is not regulated by acquaintances.

One is inevitably reminded of the young Irving writing to Florence O'Callaghan: 'Say of her to me, Flo, what you will – I willingly accept it but sayings or opinions of others keep back – especially expressions of condescension. These I cannot endure.' And: 'I hope my dearest with all my soul that when the day is past an end will be put to all reproaches from you or misunderstandings by me. . . . You still love me as you did – don't you my darling? *Answer this.*'

The situation of the two young men was very different because Tree and Maud Holt sincerely loved each other and theirs was to be a lifelong partnership in marriage and on the stage; but there is a dignity and a proper wilfulness in the letters of each which adds nobility to their relations with the two rebellious young women, and which allows us to comprehend why, in turn, they were to head their profession.

Tree's letter was written while Maud was away in Aix-les-Bains looking after a sick sister. Before he had time to post it he received a telegram from her saying: 'Come if like directly.' He then enclosed what he had written with another letter in which he said: 'Since writing this, I have received your telegram. I shall come to you at once. Nevertheless, I think it right to send this letter.' He then hurried to Aix where in his agitation he wrote rather incoherently:

Perhaps you do not want me after my last letter. – Anyhow, it may be that it would be preferred that I should not see you. If this is so I will not trouble you – I will not inflict myself on you, and if you will only give me a hint I will leave by the very first train. . . . Anyhow I only intended making a very short stay. – I did not wish to be unkind in saying what I did in my last letter to you – but it will be much better for us all not to be undecided any longer. . . . I don't know what to do or say – I wish the two hours of suspense were over. Don't hesitate to do whatever you think for the best. H.

This touching appeal could hardly fail in its effect and the two spent happy days in Aix together. Later, however, Maud Holt took exception to Tree's friendship with E. W. Godwin, the architect and stage designer, whose many amorous affairs had come to her ears. Once more Tree issued an ultimatum; once more she accepted it, and it was not long before the little half-brother waited under the rustic arches to act as best man. 'When at last he appeared . . .' Max wrote later, 'he looked so pale and excited that I gasped out instinctively: "Have you lost the ring?" I felt, god though he was, that it would be rather like him to have lost the ring.' And for proof that marriage brought tolerance to the bride, we have a letter from her husband written when she was away from home in which he remarks casually: 'The guests, Vezin, Godwin and Claud Ponsonby, have just departed. – We have had a pleasant chatty evening – plenty of scandal, you may imagine. – The corpses of soda water bottles and those of departed spirits are strewn around me, and I am alone.'

It was the custom to say of Tree that as an actor he remained an amateur all his life. By this was meant not that the effects he achieved were amateurish but that he could not repeat them again and again. Henry Irving was self-taught, as Tree was, but he acquired a control that enabled him to seize on and fix a movement or a tone of voice, so that, without recapturing the emotion that first inspired it, he could reproduce it every night for weeks. Tree seems never to have wished to learn this technique and he approached his parts afresh every night. This must have made him a difficult actor to play with but it saved him, as Bernard Shaw said, from staleness and provoked in him, as in Viola Tree's account of his scene with her in *Richard II*, a spontaneous response to the other actors in the play. This lack of technique unfitted him for certain parts as for instance where long sustained passages made it necessary to devise and then learn a method of breathing, but it did nothing to diminish the impact he made on the stage. Max Beerbohm who, in his capacity as dramatic critic to the *Saturday Review*, never wrote about his brother, tells us in his memoir that even as a child he could see 'the enormous difference between him and the ordinary "sound" actor, and why it was that his fame was so great, and always becoming greater.'

Tree was pre-eminent as a character actor because he had the ability to transform his whole personality and appearance so that it often happened that he came on to the stage unrecognised. He did this without tremendously heavy make-up but by a mental and physical, an internal and external, assumption of the role he was to perform. Louis Parker says that when it became known that Tree would play Beethoven many people doubted his ability to do it because of the physical differences: Beethoven was short and stocky with dark eyes. Then he says: 'I shall never forget our gasp of surprise when Tree made his first entrance at the dress-rehearsal: a short, stocky, square-set little man, with dark eyes. His head was Beethoven's head. I have two portraits before me as I write: one of Beethoven and one of Tree in the part, and it is difficult to tell which is which.' However Bernard Shaw did not admire Tree as a character actor and he once wrote:

His *tours de force* in the art of make-up do not impose on me: any man can get into a wicker barrel and pretend to be Falstaff, or put on a false nose and call himself Svengali. Such tricks may very well be left to the music-halls: they are altogether unworthy of an artist of Mr Tree's pretensions. When he returns to the serious pursuit of his art by playing a part into which he can sincerely enter without disguise or mechanical denaturalization, may I be there to see! Until then let him guard the Haymarket doors against me; for I like him best when he is most himself.

The evidence is very strong, however, that this critical treatment of Tree as a character actor was due to a want of appreciation in Shaw rather than to a failure in Tree. Max Beerbohm wrote to Hesketh Pearson:

Shaw's remark about Herbert's *métier* being 'straight parts' seems to me to be great nonsense. I remember he once said to me that Herbert wasn't really a comedian, but a romantic actor – a theory which I flatly rejected. Herbert had of course a strong element of romance, but the main thing about him was that he was an immensley versatile and *richly creative* comedian.

And after quoting this passage Pearson adds: 'The truth is that Tree was equally successful in character comedy and quiet pathos. Where he failed completely was in purely romantic work, of which he gave the worst example in 1892 when he produced *Hamlet*.'

Desmond MacCarthy's account of Tree acting is by far the best, most sympathetic and most perceptive account left to us. He tells us that Tree was essentially 'a romantic actor, perhaps the last exuberant descendant of Romanticism flowering on the English stage'. And again that 'in judging his talent and in placing him among his predecessors and contemporaries, it is important to think of him as an actor trailing with him into the twentieth century clouds of romanticism, from which, for our eyes, the glow and colour had in a measure departed.' Then he goes on to say that, if Tree was pre-eminently a romantic, the next thing to note about him is that he was a character actor. 'A character actor is one that does not excel chiefly in playing certain recurring situations, but in building up before our eyes a definite human being. Tree possessed the power of conceiving character in a very high degree. Of all his contemporaries he had the largest share of this author's gift.' But he goes on to say that an actor must have also the faculty of representing the characters he understands and that Tree's power of understanding character often outran his power of representing it.

He could make himself look like Falstaff; he understood and revelled in the character of Falstaff, but his performance lacked fundamental force. Hence the contradiction in his acting: his performance as a whole often fell short of high excellence, yet these same impersonations were lit by insight and masterly strokes of interpretation, which made the spectator feel that he was watching the performance of the most imaginative of living actors.

MacCarthy tells us that Tree was always better in representing weakness than strength – 'failure whether of the faithful or ignoble kind' – and that he was 'admirable in the expression of that irony which is the revenge of the beaten or the refuge of the helpless'.

One characteristic of his acting – and it distinguished him from most of his eminent contemporaries – was that he always acted from his imagination. He flung himself neck and crop into his parts. Sometimes the results were disasterous, but even on these occasions there was always discernible that effort to become entirely the part which is the foundation of good acting.

And, most revealing of all, Desmond MacCarthy tells us this:

He was pre-eminently a social man, not a solitary one. He had that temperament which saves a man from becoming a crank, but at the same time makes it hard for him to trust those slight evanescent promptings which must be listened for and obeyed, if he is to find himself completely as an artist. Although he had obviously plenty of confidence and courage in undertaking the most diverse parts, I doubt if he had in him that hard kernel of arrogance which has made it easier for less gifted, less original men to get the best and only the best, out of themselves.

Herbert Tree made his first big hit as the Rev. Robert Spalding in *The Private Secretary*. He was under contract to a man named Edgar Bruce who let his theatre and his company with it to Charles Hawtrey. Tree was outraged at having to play this part and as a protest he deliberately burlesqued it, inventing much business and many gags. But these were so successful that they were taken over by W. S. Penley, the actor who afterwards played the part again and again and later became the original Charley's Aunt. Tree himself left *The Private Secretary* to play an Italian spy in a thriller, and with his performance of this very dissimilar part, his reputation was made.

Unlike Forbes-Robertson, who went into management because he felt it forced upon him, or Irving who did so to produce the plays that gave him the greatest opportunity as an actor, Tree was attracted to management for its own sake and remarking that 'Everything comes to him who doesn't wait', he took a theatre of his own at the earliest opportunity. In 1887, at the age of thirty-five and with the financial backing of a friend, he opened in management at the Comedy Theatre in Panton Street in a play called *The Red Lamp*. Tree played Demetrius, the head of the secret police, and when he came on to the stage made up to represent this character he did so unrecognised. 'Ripened judgment [Max Beerbohm was later to write] has not inclined me to think *The Red Lamp* the greatest play ever written. But I thought it so on its first night – the first night of Herbert's management. And I saw it seventeen times, without changing my opinion.'

Following the success of *The Red Lamp* Tree took the Haymarket Theatre and there followed one of those long settled periods, like the period of the Bancroft management, which has made this historic theatre one of the most famous in London.

Tree was beyond everything else a man of the theatre, one of those who find romance and fulfilment quite as much in the long stone corridors to the dressing-rooms, the voice of the call-boy, the mechanism of the scene shifts and the lighting, the vaulting shadows behind and the artificial brilliance in front of the sets, all the paraphernalia of stage-craft, as in the applause of the audiences. Consequently, his first allegiance was to the theatre, not to himself, and, unlike Irving, who required only 'table legs' to support the central figure, he engaged the best actors and actresses he could find and gave them the greatest opportunity. Bernard Shaw, in a letter to Ellen Terry, wrote that Tree 'surrounds himself with counter-attractions and lets them play him off the stage to their heart's content as long as he takes the money at the doors'. And, although Ellen Terry characteristically replied: 'You think Tree "lets the rest of his company play him off the stage"! I'd like you to see what is written in his heart upon that subject,' he insisted that Lewis

Waller, playing with Tree, was 'ten times as good as the very best man you have supporting Henry at the Lyceum. He has authority, self-respect, dignity, and often brilliancy: you do not see him dodging about the stage with one eye on "the governor".'

Tree also had a greater literary taste than was common in the theatre at that time. He was always on the look-out for plays of some real quality; it was he who produced *Beau Austin*, and who suggested to W. E. Henley and Robert Louis Stevenson that they write a new version of the old melodrama *Robert Macaire* – plays which caused Max Beerbohm to give the whole of one week's article in the *Saturday Review* to the problem: What precisely was Mr Henley's share in the plays done jointly by Robert Louis Stevenson and himself? His speculations upon the point, as on all others, should be read for themselves. What is certain is that Tree as well as Henley had some share in the new version of *Macaire*.

I suggested to them [he wrote] to make Robert Macaire a philosopher in crime. . . . I made a number of suggestions for the play and they wrote it, offering that I should be a part author. . . . This I declined – as I had done nothing. . . . I had occasion to regret my modesty, for when we came to produce the play I wanted to make some alterations, as I considered the construction somewhat faulty. My suggestions were pooh-poohed. The play was produced and the notices given to my performance were more flattering than were the references to the play. . . . Henley wrote to me somewhat violently, saying I had evidently done the butter-slide trick with the play; to which I replied that if he would not cease his correspondence I would do the play no more. . . . Still I have always liked him in spite of his bludgeonesque manners. One day I met him in the street in Edinburgh. He asked me, 'Why did you not come to see me?' To which I replied, 'My dear Henley, I forgot for the moment that we were on speaking terms.'

Hesketh Pearson said of Tree that he was 'the father of the repertory movement'. Quite early in his management he gave a series of Monday evening and Wednesday afternoon performances of plays – such as *Beau Austin* – which he thought could not be played as a commercial proposition. In spite of Irving's many successes it was still believed that 'Shakespeare spells ruin' and Tree originally put on *The Merry Wives of*

Windsor at one of these extra performances. In 1888, however, it went into the evening bill and was so frequently revived that Falstaff became one of Tree's most popular parts.

'When is repertory not repertory?' he asked. 'When it is a success.'

With the great success of *The Merry Wives of Windsor* it became apparent that Tree was becoming a potential rival to Irving. It was commonly believed that Irving watched the advance of the younger man with jealousy and several rather grim stories are told as evidence that he entertained this unbecoming emotion. In a play called *The Village Priest*, produced at the Haymarket, an actor named Charles Allan, who had been a member of the Lyceum company, made a single entrance and spoke the words 'Allons! Marche'. When Irving went round to see Tree after watching the play he talked lightly for some time and on taking his leave said with obvious embarrassment: 'Good-night – hm – Allen   excellent – hm – God bless you!' And ten years later a friend of Irving's described sitting with him while, at the close of Act 2 of a play called *Herod*, Tree in the leading part ascended an imposing bronze staircase, reciting the names of the places recently added to his dominions.

> Hippo, Samaria and Gadara,
> And Gaza unto these, and Straton's tower.
> And high-walled Joppa, and Anthedon's shore,

'Well,' Irving's friend asked, 'What do you think of that?' And Irving replied:

'Ah! Hm. . . . A very fine flight of steps.'

It is probably, nevertheless, an over-simplification to describe the emotions Irving felt as jealousy. When he went to see his own son H. B. Irving play Hamlet, a production in which a brazier was placed on the battlements, the only thing he could find to say was: 'I see – me boy – the streets are up in Elsinore.'

And, although in one case he was watching one of the leading actors of his day and in the other the early efforts of a youth who was to become a good but never a great actor, it seems likely that to Irving they were both men whose performances to his embarrassment he could not praise. It is very common for interpretative artists, musicians as well as actors,

to be unable to see any merit in the performance of a contemporary. Having, after long years of study and experience,
achieved a rendering of a role or a piece of music which,
while giving the greatest play to their own talents, adds the
sum of these talents to the genius of the composer, they cannot
consider a rendering which is quite different equally valid and
illuminating. A certain integrity to their art forbids them prais-
ing what they cannot like and makes them feel resentful that
anything so unworthy should be successful. In many artists this
impervious shell or arrogance is a constituent of the single-
minded devotion which enables them to give the fullest expression to their own gifts. Irving was undoubtedly one of these.
He seldom visited the theatre, often giving offence because he
failed in the courtesy of going to see foreign actors in London.

However, Irving had no reason to be jealous of Tree's Hamlet,
which was generally regarded as a failure. Tree had neither the
technique nor the temperament for Hamlet and he surprised
the more intelligent play-goers even of his own day by returning unseen by Ophelia after the scene in which he rages at
her to kiss a tress of her hair.

'I never saw anything so funny in my life,' W. S. Gilbert said
of his performance, 'and yet it was not in the least vulgar' (a
phrase which Hesketh Pearson believes led to the common
form 'funny without being vulgar').

In 1895 Tree was responsible for the first production of A
Woman of No Importance and, when he gave a matinée of
An Enemy of the People, for the first performance of an Ibsen
play by a leading West End management. The second of these
plays was sufficiently well-received to be revived occasionally
and the first was very successful. Desmond MacCarthy says of
An Enemy of the People that it was an example both of his
weakness as a producer and of his gift for comprehending
character. To liven up the play he introduced some completely
inappropriate foolery, but his own acting as Dr Stockmann
was 'masterly and subtle'.

He was perfect in the impassioned, indignant harangues, in
representing Stockmann's incredulous distress of mind, his readiness to drop any number of points if only people will listen, a
readiness which looks so like want of dignity but springs from sin-
cerity. . . . That Tree comprehended his character completely was

shown in the way he brought out to perfection that rare and touching humour which expresses itself in ways and words so like those of a person who has no humour, that people without a sense of character do not see the difference.

And Hesketh Pearson tells us that Tree was very good as Lord Illingworth in *A Woman of No Importance*, liking the part so much that he began to throw off his own witticisms in the same style. 'Every day,' Wilde remarked, 'dear Herbert becomes *de plus en plus Oscarisé*; it is a wonderful case of Nature imitating Art.'

Pearson says, too, that Wilde and Tree were in some respects very much alike. Both possessed happy natures, enjoyed life and revelled in nonsense. Both laughed at their own jokes as much as at other people's and both loved good food, good wine and good company. One might add that both were kind and both possessed an element of fantasy in their wit, in pursuit of which both could be very silly.

In January 1895 Tree took his company to America. Here, although he and Mrs Tree had an overwhelming social success, he was not immediately acclaimed by the critics and the public as Irving had been. He had a slightly guttural accent and eccentricities of manner and the American public did not take to him completely until he was nearing the end of his life. This did not in any way affect his own enjoyment or his liking for the place. Max Beerbohm accompanied him on this first tour as his private secretary with salary. ('But my mission was rather a failure. The letters that I wrote in his stead were so carefully thought out and worded that many of the letters sent to him could get no answer at all.') He has recorded that his brother was instantly responsive to the magic of New York.

While Tree was playing in Philadelphia a very successful dramatic version by Paul Potter of George du Maurier's best-selling novel, *Trilby*, was being played at one of the other theatres. Tree sent his brother to see and report on this. Across the supper-table that night Max reported to the effect that 'the play in itself was utter nonsense and could only be a dismal failure in London'. Six weeks later in New York, having one free evening before he sailed, Tree went to see *Trilby* himself.

At the end of the second act he left his box, found Paul Poter and purchased the English rights of the play. The name *Trilby* was to acquire the same association with that of Tree as *The Bells* with that of Irving; and, although Tree's American tour had not been a great financial success in itself, he carried home with him, like the scrip of shares in a gold mine, the foundation of a fortune.

Trilby, which in George du Maurier's own version is a minor classic, is the story of a girl who, though possessing the chest and vocal cords of a singer – the instrument of a voice – is totally unmusical and unable to sing in tune. She comes under the influence of Svengali, a musician and a hypnotist, and under his spell becomes a world famous singer. 'Svengali's make-up is marvellous,' W. S. Gilbert wrote to Maud Tree. 'We could *smell* him.' Hesketh Pearson gives the following account:

It was astonishing how Tree with the utmost economy of means could alter the entire appearance of his face. 'It takes father far less time to make himself ugly than it takes mother to make herself beautiful!' said Viola. No one could account for the celerity with which it was done or the amazing effectiveness of the result. While Irving used to spend an hour or more to make himself look like another edition of Irving, Tree transformed himself completely in ten minutes. Yet, though the Svengali disguise was remarkable, the performance was an epitome of Treeisms: the quick slinking walk, the flashing eyes, the hand on hip, the fluttering fingers, the foreign gestures, the slightly guttural accents: in this part even his faults were turned into virtues, and the total mesmeric effect, as if Trilby's singing entirely resulted from Svengali's power, was a triumph of suggestion.

George du Maurier had himself illustrated his novel and the public had a perfectly clear idea of what Trilby should look like. Tree had to find a young actress who must be tall and beautiful and sufficiently like the du Maurier drawings. From the start everything boded well for this venture and an eighteen-year-old girl named Dorothea Baird was discovered who, although inexperienced, was almost ideal for the part.[2] *Trilby* had an immediate success at its first production in Manchester, ran for many months at the Haymarket, was revived again

---

[2] Dorothea Baird married H. B. Irving and was the mother of Sir Henry Irving's biographer, Laurence Irving.

and again and was an enormous money-maker. Tree had himself written two of the scenes for the London version and, as
Hesketh Pearson has already pointed out, Shaw showed his
acuteness in immediately picking out one of these. 'I derived
much cynical amusement from this most absurd scene; but if
I were Mr du Maurier, I should ask whether the theatre is
really in such an abject condition that all daintiness and serious-
ness of thought and feeling must be struck out of a book, and
replaced by vulgar nonsense before it can be accepted on the
stage.' This lends interest to Tree's often-quoted estimate of the
play, given to someone who praised it to him. 'Hogwash,' he
is said to have replied. But it is very doubtful whether an actor
can successfully write and play in scenes which to his taste are
hogwash. It seems likely that Tree, who revelled in his part
and in the play, took his intellectual estimate of it from, among
other people, his brother, Max.

Tree's liking for management for its own sake became pre-
dominant in his character as he grew older. He had the reckless
magnificence and the comprehensive creative ambition of the
true impresario. Every day as he arrived at the Haymarket he
could see on the other side of the street the site on which Sir
John Vanbrugh had once designed and managed a theatre, at
present occupied by an old opera house which was shortly to
be demolished. Even before the success of *Trilby* he had determined to acquire this site and build his own theatre there, and
the fortune made by this play enabled him to put £10,000 into
the enterprise. Others who put up money were Sir Ernest
Cassel and Lord Rothschild.[3]

Her Majesty's Theatre (renamed His Majesty's after the death
of Queen Victoria) was built in Portland stone by C. J. Phipps
with interior decorations by Romaine-Walker, and when it
was finished Bernard Shaw wrote:

It rises spaciously and brilliantly to the dignity of art; and if its
way of doing so is still elegantly rhetorical and Renascent in conception, yet that style is not altogether the wrong one for a theatre;

[3] Hesketh Pearson tells us that the enterprise was financed by a company called The
Playhouse Ltd, the capital consisting of debentures, and that Tree's debentures ranked
after the others for the payment of interest. He says that Tree paid just under £6,000
a year ground rent and the building, estimated at £55,000, cost very little more.

and it is wonderfully humanized and subtilized by the influence of modern anti-Renaissance ideas on the decoration. . . . The Lyceum and Drury Lane, old as they are, would, if they were destroyed, be regretted as the Garrick and Daly's would never be regretted, but not more than Her Majesty's, which has as yet no associations.

Her Majesty's Theatre was for Herbert Tree the richest reward of his life. It realised his dreams, and it became not merely the scene of his creative triumphs, the spur of his ambition, but his solace from pain, his refuge from society, and at times his home. He built two rooms for himself in the great dome, one of which was, like the Beefsteak Room at the Lyceum under Irving, the scene of magnificent hospitality and small intimate dinners, the other a study and bedroom combined. Viola Tree tells us that he hoped the bronze dome would turn green. They used to look up at it together from the top of the Haymarket and one or other of them would remark: 'I think it's a little greener today, don't you?'

The banqueting hall under the dome was a high room ending in rafters. The small inner room had a frieze running round it with scenes from *Twelfth Night*, *The Tempest* and *The Taming of the Shrew*. Underneath these were bookshelves containing, his daughter says, 'great big useful books' and a mass of hopeless presentation copies bearing such titles as 'Shakespeare Through an Old Stagers' Spectacles', while the interesting books and papers were piled up on chairs, sofas, desks. And she tells us he loved the theatre.

He loved the place, and never could keep away from it for long. Even on my wedding day, when we were driving to St. Martin's Church, I very typical and rather sedate (for me), with veil and train poised ready for my spring on to the red carpet, he turned to me suddenly in Regent Street and said, 'Will you drive me down to the theatre, first, dear?' And so at the stage-door I, the bride, sat watching his beloved figure – flamboyant coat-tails, hat, stick and all – vanish through the swing doors, only to return a few minutes later having found out that all was well. I was so glad afterwards, as it would not have seemed natural for me to be driving with him and not to stop there.

And Iris Tree wrote at the same time:

Theatres have lost their meaning for me now – I have known one theatre so well, and have loved it so long, it has run through the chain of all my memories, but now the link is broken. When I was a child the theatre was a refuge from lessons, mutton and rain, a place whose mystery was never dimmed by familiarity, a place of sliding curtains and endless doors, a corridor of echoing adventures.

Her Majesty's is a big theatre – too big many people thought to suit the subtle delineations of human sensibility and emotion in which Tree excelled. In it he gave vent to the exuberant and theatrical side of his nature which made him so much enjoy management. Although he produced many plays by other authors, his years at Her Majesty's were chiefly notable for his Shakespearian productions, and these for the magnificence and extravagance of detail with which they were presented. Hesketh Pearson wrote, in a comparison scarcely complimentary to either actor: 'In the presentation of Shakespeare, as opposed to the exploitation of an actor's individuality, Tree must be given the palm. His acting versions were as much like the original texts *as the elaborate scenery allowed*. whereas Irving's had been arranged to exhibit the leading actor.'[4]

In defence of both actors it must be said that they drew crowds into the theatre to see Shakespeare at a time when he was held to 'spell ruin' – something no one else would attempt in the West End of London until 1925, when John Barrymore proved once more that it could be done by playing *Hamlet* to full houses at the Haymarket.[5]

Tree's first Shakespearian production at Her Majesty's was of *Julius Caesar*. The scenery and costumes were by Laurence Alma-Tadema and the acting of a quality to inspire Shaw's remarks to Ellen Terry quoted on p. 153. Tree played Antony, and there was general agreement that it was both the most magnificently mounted and the best acted production of Shakespeare within living memory. It was fifty years since *Julius Caesar* had been seen in the West End and it ran for five months and made a profit of £11,000. *Twelfth Night*, Pearson tells us, was Tree's most satisfactory Shakespearian production, Olivia's garden being copied from a photograph in *Country Life* and

---

[4] My italics.

[5] Barrymore, John, 1882–1942. The cast for his *Hamlet* at the Haymarket included Constance Collier as Gertrude and Fay Compton as Ophelia.

being both beautiful and realistic. Tree played Malvolio with much invention of comic business and with four little Malvolios who followed him about and lined up behind him whenever he spoke. This business was sufficiently successful for Tree's half-brother to write to his biographer after his death : 'His Svengali and his Malvolio abide in my mind as two of his especial triumphs.'

In the opening scene of *The Tempest* a ship rocked on a realistic sea, the waves splashed and the wind roared; in *Antony and Cleopatra* the text had to be re-arranged to suit the scenery, the return of Antony to Alexandria, which is the occasion of one speech in the text, being illustrated by a tableau in which excited crowds and dancing girls were a prelude to the arrival to music, first of Cleopatra, then of Anthony. In *Richard II* real horses were introduced in the Lists at Coventry, and Tree as Richard entered London on a horse in place of the speech in which the Duke of York merely describes this happening.

The result of all this accumulation of commentary and illustration [Desmond MacCarthy wrote] however ingenious or lavish, round a play was often to slow down its action intolerably; and while attempting to interpret Shakespeare to the eye, the production too often failed to interpret him to the mind. Thus it was that, in company with several other critics, I found myself, when Shakespeare was on at His Majesty's, shouting : 'Sir Herbert Tree's carriage stops the way !'

But the public continued to fill the theatre and Tree to be unmoved by criticism. People who did not like theatrical illusion, he said, need not come to the theatre. 'The bookworm has always his book.'

When Tree was a young man Dion Boucicault expressed surprise that he should know so well the tricks of the trade.

'Mention one trick,' Tree said.

'You allow the gestures to precede the words.'

'Do I?' said Tree. 'Well, I'm sorry you told me, for now I shall probably do it all wrong.'

And he said once : 'I have not got technique. It is a dull thing; it enslaves the imagination.'

It is strange that a man who believed these things should

have been the founder of the Royal Academy of Dramatic Art. In 1904 Tree took and furnished two houses in Gower Street and started a school which taught elocution, dancing and fencing. He then lent his theatre for public performance by the students, gave advice when asked for it and jobs to the most promising pupils. His academy filled a much felt need and it prospered so greatly that it soon became a national institution.

At the same time he initiated an annual Shakespearian festival at Her Majesty's putting on six plays in six days in all the splendour of their original productions. In 1909 he received a knighthood for his services as an actor and manager, and in 1910 he put on *Henry VII*, which was generally regarded as the most magnificent of all his productions and which in the early days of the war was finally to ensure his complete triumph over American audiences.

It would be wrong, however, to conceive the programme of plays put on at Her Majesty's in terms of one Shakespearian production after another, because Tree, like everyone else, produced a great many purely commercial plays that have no abiding interest and a few – such as the Henley-Stevenson *Macaire, Trilby, Beau Austin*, a version of *Oliver Twist* in which he made a marvellous Fagin and a Christmas play by Graham Robertson called *Pinkie and the Fairies* – which some people still remember. The only plays still regularly performed to which he gave a first performance are *A Woman of No Importance* and *Pygmalion*.

Rehearsals under Tree's management were well known for their chaotic character. An unmotivated anarchy reigned, people came in and out of the theatre, sat and talked to Tree, who every now and then produced a witticism at which he and all his henchmen laughed, the stage staff rushed about in all directions, people bellowed at each other and stood distractedly about. At one rehearsal, overcome by the attempts of his stage-manager to impose some order on the scene, Tree knelt and prayed: 'Dear Lord, do look at Bertie Shelton *now*.' There is no explanation of what magic ultimately restored order in time for the curtain to go up on the vastly complicated and magnificent scenes for which this theatre was famous. Tree was not at all quarrelsome by nature, but he quarrelled at rehearsals with Henry Arthur Jones (who quarrelled with a great many other people), with Mrs Patrick Campbell (who sometimes managed to drive him screaming from the stage), and he went very near quarrelling with Shaw. Shaw said afterwards that he could never bring himself to hit Tree hard enough – 'whereas no poker was thick enough, no brick heavy enough, to leave a bruise on Mrs Campbell'. He said also that the effect of rehearsing under Tree's management became apparent to him only when he saw some photographs of himself after the first night. He suppressed these but he sent one to Mrs Campbell saying 'Are you not ashamed?' and another to Tree saying 'This is your work.'

Tree made £13,000 out of the first production of *Pygmalion*; he took it off when it was still making a great deal of money because he was bored with it and wanted a holiday, and also because Shaw's lack of interest in his performance irritated him. Out of self-preservation Shaw refused to see the play until the hundredth performance, when he discovered without surprise that Tree had introduced a happy ending by throwing a bunch of flowers to Eliza in the interval between the end of the play and the fall of the curtain.

'My ending makes money : you ought to be grateful,' said Tree afterwards.

'Your ending is damnable : you ought to be shot,' Shaw replied.

All this happened in the summer of 1914.

Tree had a talent for neat little aphorisms with which he amused himself so much that he would sometimes call out to his secretary to make a note of something he had just said, or, when reminded of some earlier saying, cry delightedly : 'Did I say that? Did I say that?' Too many of his sayings which require the occasion and the glowing personality for a just appreciation have been preserved in print. But in addition to wit Tree had the masculine virtues of tolerance and generosity which are reflected in the following endearing examples of these sayings :

It is better to drink a little too much than much too little.

And of marriage :

Which is the victim – he or she – She was, he is.

The second of these has a sad truth which, while of general application, had a particular reference to his own case. For Tree was as incapable of fidelity as his wife was of condoning infidelity.

The picture that is left to us of Maud Tree is less attractive than she may have been in her lifetime. In the first place we have the series of letters written to her by Tree during their engagement which show her in a harsh and puritan light, in the second she had not the gift of easy self-expression which he possessed and passed on to his children. Consequently, the long essay she wrote in the collection of memories of her husband is not only the least satisfactory in the book but probably does less than justice to herself. For if it is true that writers with the gift of style can preserve for us the quality and individuality of men long dead, it is equally true that a false picture can endure through the lack of it.

There are varying accounts of her ability as an actress, but Bernard Shaw suprisingly tells us that she was a natural comedian. She seems also to have been a wit and some of her sayings, like those of her husband, have been the rounds. Of these the most apt was when Tree, having persuaded Mrs Kendal and Ellen Terry rather late in the careers of these two great actresses to appear as Mistress Ford and Mistress Page to his Falstaff, came into the theatre together with them.

'Look at Herbert and his two stars,' someone remarked.

'Two ancient lights,' Maud Tree replied.[6]

The Trees' married life had to survive the difficulties caused by her acting in his company.

'*Why* Marion Terry? *Why* not me?' she asked him once. And received the reply:

'You see, the part needs extraordinary sympathy.'

But Tree's great kindness, generosity and affection might have been enough to appease her for his lack of prejudice as a manager had he not transgressed so audaciously and so frequently as a husband that, feeling herself too much sinned against, she failed in all those qualities of sweetness, good temper and tolerance in which he so conspicuously shone.

---

[6] The story is also told of Irving who, passing the theatre and seeing on the bills Mrs Tree's name together with Mrs Kendal's and Ellen Terry's, remarked to his companion: 'Three little meds [maids] – eh! Three little meds.'

This classical situation was completed by Tree's unequivocal resentment when Lewis Waller fell in love with his wife, and for a few years the Trees did each other so much damage when together that they seldom met. Then Maud Tree, out for a drive with Lewis Waller (whose love, it was believed, she accepted with gratitude but did not return), had an accident and broke her jaw. This spoiled her appearance and ended her career. She suffered deeply, and in this situation Tree's sympathy and affection were so necessary to her and so overwhelming that she ceased to do violence to his angelic qualities in an effort to retain a monopoly of them. She reconciled herself to the fact of his natural sons and learned to make jokes about his susceptibilities. Tree adored his children and in all ways but the one was a family man. 'Be sweet, dearest Viola,' he wrote to his daughter, 'during all the years, as you have been to me during all the years that have passed. Your fond Father. And do remember to spell holiday with one "l"!' During his last years he managed to enjoy the society and affection of all his loved ones and, when his daughter Iris was to meet one of her half-brothers, it was her mother whom Tree asked to explain the situation to her.

The Great War of 1914 sent audiences into the theatres with a taste for only the lightest of fare. After two failures in London Tree went to Hollywood to make a film of *Macbeth*, letting His Majesty's Theatre to Oscar Asche. Asche produced a musical play called *Chu Chin Chow* which occupied the theatre for five years – at that time the longest run in history. Tree put on a Shakespearian season in New York, playing *Henry VIII*, *The Merchant of Venice* and *The Merry Wives of Windsor*. He had an enormous success and wrote to his wife: 'They want me to have a theatre here in the autumn and call it the Tree Theatre.' He made speeches from the stage and elsewhere in aid of the Allied cause and on one occasion he gave a performance of *Oliver Twist* for the benefit of the Red Cross in which the Artful Dodger was played by Charlie Chaplin. Then he made a triumphant tour of all the leading cities of America with his Shakespearian productions, making speeches wherever he went and earning from the *New York Times* the title of 'unofficial ambassador extraordinary'. In 1916 and again in 1917 he faced the hazards of an Atlantic crossing to visit England.

Max Beerbohm believed that in the last years of his life his brother grew to care less for acting.

His versatility had ranged over so vast a number of diverse interpretations. What new thing was there for him to do – for him, to whom the notion of marking time was so utterly repugnant? Especially after the outbreak of the War did I notice in him an impatience of his work. The last time we met was at my mother's house, just after his return from America. He was looking, as usual, splendidly well, and was full of animation. But in all his talk there was not a word about acting.

In the summer of 1917 Tree was staying at Epple Bay in Birchington when he slipped and fell down the stairs. He had a successful operation on his knee but blood clots formed as a result of it. He died at the age of 64, his personal radiance undimmed. He was a very great actor and one of the last truly romantic figures. Stick in hand and coat tails swinging, he dominated the theatrical scene for many years. For all who can remember his name the very words 'actor-manager' recall it. 'Irving,' one says, 'and Tree.'

Sir Gerald du Maurier
1873-1933

Gerald du Maurier was a fine late flowering of the genus, highly and subtly developed. In point of time he has no place in this book because, although he started his career on the stage in the nineteenth century, he did not go into management until 1910. Yet, although a man of the twentieth century, more precisely one who took colour from both and gave it to the period between the wars, his affinity to the Victorian actor-managers was unquestionable. During his long period at Wyndham's he was not a manager in the true sense of being responsible for the finance of the theatre. He entered into an arrangement with Frank Curzon by which the latter supplied him with a theatre, a fixed income and a percentage of the profits. Curzon took all the financial risks but did not interfere with the policy or the choice or presentation of the plays. For twenty-five years Gerald du Maurier's name was connected with Wyndham's Theatre, as Irving's had been with the Lyceum, Alexander's with the St James's and Tree's with Her Majesty's.

Du Maurier was the subject of one of the most famous biographies in theatrical history, written by his daughter, Daphne, soon after his death. Chiefly remembered for a style which, very individual and in itself short-lived, killed forever the old romantic style of acting, he was, nevertheless, the last of the romantic heroes of the theatre.

He was born unusually well-equipped for the stage. His lean, brown, rather crooked face with the jutting chin and the brushed-back hair was oddly beautiful, witty, sensitive and rather cruel; formed, as Shaw said of Ellen Terry's, in a unique mould. He recalled no other person, conformed to no general type. He put his natural elegance to the service of his casual, throw-away manner, partly invented, partly absorbed from the trivial manner of the day, but this did not diminish the impact of his personality. He had all the magnetism and easy dominance of his great predecessors.

The son of a man whose fame, although not earned in the theatre, had spilled over into it, Gerald du Maurier acquired no added grace from a pseudonym. He bore easily and artlessly the name of a French family of minor nobility and it was not until after his death that Miss Daphne du Maurier discovered and published the fact that he owed it to one of the many fantasies of his great-grandfather. Robert-Mathurin Busson came to London at the time of the French revolution, not, as he pretended, to escape the fate of an aristocrat, but after suffering one prison sentence for fraud and in fear of another. He was obsessed with social status and delusions of grandeur and in London, where poverty in an emigré family was not unusual, he was able to invent for himself a claim to nobility. He began to sign himself Busson du Maurier and, when he discovered that there was a real Comte du Maurier living in La Sarthe, he fabricated a story of relationship and intermarriage between the Aubreys, the family of the real counts, and the Bussons, so that the chateau at le Maurier and the family living there made his stories seem more rather than less probable to later generations.

Robert-Mathurin Busson was the father of six children, of whom one, Louis Mathurin, married an Englishwoman named Ellen Clarke, the daughter of a famous Regency courtesan who was mistress of Frederick, Duke of York. These two were the parents of George du Maurier.

George du Maurier, born in 1834, lived part of his childhood in London, part in Paris. Thus the duality of his inheritance was repeated in his environment. As a young man he studied art but owing to the loss of the sight of one eye had to give up any idea of working as a painter and to earn his living as an illustrator. This was at a time when illustration was regarded as an art requiring specialised talents and du Maurier, who was on the staff of Punch with Charles Keene and John Tenniel, first made his name with his drawings. Later in life be began to write novels and his second book, Trilby, was the first 'best-seller' in England and in America. He was an admirable artist in both mediums. His *Punch* drawings are a major source for social historians and, if the enormous sales of *Trilby* can be accounted for more by the Svengali theme than by the wit and charm of the earlier part of the book, Svengali had sufficient originality and power to become an authentic literary figure. The gift of romantic, rather sentimental story-telling is an important part of the heritage of the du Maurier family.

George du Maurier was very light-hearted and gay in society and a tremendous talker. He had a really fine tenor voice and a talent for singing French songs. Nick-named Kicky, he was very much loved and a list of his friends and well-known acquaintances would be a list of the artists and literary figures of the period. At the same time, his biographer tells us, 'his status as a gentleman was quite secure, and he was able to mix in the best society'. He was a close friend of Henry James.

When he first joined *Punch* he received instructions from Mark Lemon, a famous editor who understood the talents of his contributors. 'I was particularly told not to try to be broadly funny, but to undertake the light and graceful business, like a *jeune premier*.' Among the talents which the highly talented Kicky was to pass to his talented son, that for 'the light and graceful business' was supreme.

Yet he suffered from what his latest biographer describes as the 'aching nostalgia' to which Ruskin was also prone. She states that: 'Continual backward looking was a central feature of du Maurier's personality, the cause of much personal unhappiness, but also the source of his later creative power as a novelist.' And she quotes from *Peter Ibbetson*:

Oh, surely, surely, I cried to myself, we ought to find some means of possessing the past more fully and completely than we do. Life is not worth living for many of us if a want so desperate and yet so natural can never be satisfied. Memory is but a poor, rudimentary thing that we had better be without, if it can only lead us to the verge of consummation like this, and madden us with a desire it cannot slake.

Because of his eyes he could never escape from the dread of poverty and even after *Trilby* had made him a rich man he continued in fearful parsimony. In the same way when he became the anthor of a popular best-seller, his success terrified him. Leonée Ormond writes:

Like a mole, searching for dark and familiar places, du Maurier shied away from the limelight, and the public exposure to which he was subjected. The apparatus of publicity and public success, which had no note of jubilation for him, seemed to undermine his health and his confidence, to tear him from the secure and familiar patterns of his life. He was certainly suffering from fatty degeneration of the heart, but it is impossible to escape the conclusion that *Trilby*, to a very large extent, was the cause of his death.

Yet it is emphasised that it was only with the publication of *Peter Ibbetson* that the dark and melancholy side of du Maurier's nature began to be understood. Daphne du Maurier makes it plain that even his children were quite unaware of the true nature of this man.

George du Maurier married Emma Wightwick, a striking beauty but one who was always uneasy in society and cared only for her husband and her children. These she loved and tended with an anxious, passionate devotion. The du Mauriers had five children – Beatrix, Sylvia, Louise, Guy and Gerald. Gerald was the youngest and the most indulged. He was referred to in his own family as the 'ewee lamb'. He was an extremely bright, precocious child who learned very early to get his own way by playing on his mother's anxieties.

By the time of his birth in 1873 the du Mauriers were living at Hampstead, and a year later they moved into New Grove House, where they were to remain for twenty years. During almost the whole of his life Gerald du Maurier lived in Hampstead. His father used him and his brother and sisters as models for his drawings and, even when he was not drawing them, worked placidly with the five children running about in his studio.

Gerald was educated at Harrow where he did surprisingly badly in his work, his letters to his mother containing a mixture of fairly light-hearted apology for being low in his form and self-confident requests for food. 'Look here, I'm awfully sorry about tenth place but I really will do better and in the meantime will you be a darling and send down at once a large square tin of milk biscuits, a cake from Buzzards, some Cadbury's chocolate, a Roll tongue, chicken and ham sausages, two tins of sardines, some more jam and honey, and anything else you like.'

From the earliest age he mimicked the people who came to the house, and although his sisters turned away from these exhibitions remarking: 'Don't look at Gerald; he's showing off,' his father could never disguise his amusement. As he grew older he began to entertain the boys in his house at Harrow as well as his father with imitations of Henry Irving. Yet, when he left school, although he was immediately in demand for amateur theatricals, he was put to work in a shipping office. His period there was short, however, and following it he enjoyed himself for some time merely in a social way, going to dances and house-parties, always much in demand as an amateur actor. Since it soon became clear that he was not likely to make much success of anything else, his parents began to weaken in their opposition to the idea of his going on the stage. It was at this time that Henry James remarked that if Gerald really wanted to go on the stage he didn't see how his parents could prevent it.

To this du Maurier responded: 'That's all very well, James; but what would you say if you had a son who wanted to go into the church?'

Lifting both hands in horror, Henry James replied: 'My dear du Maurier, a father's curse.'

Once Gerald's parents were reconciled to the idea there was no further difficulty. George du Maurier merely applied to his friend John Hare to take the boy, and Gerald gave his first public performance in January 1894 at the Garrick Theatre as a waiter in *An Old Jew*, a comedy by Sydney Grundy. He stayed with Hare for six months, during which time he persuaded everyone of his natural talent, and then he went on tour with Forbes-Robertson, playing among other parts that of Algy in *Diplomacy*. At the end of this tour he signed a contract with Tree, with whom he stayed for two years. Much of this time was spent playing Dodor in *Trilby* since this was the period of the phenomenal success of this play. He opened with Tree in Manchester in September 1895, and after the riotous success of the provincial tour, played the part in London, in a second tour of the provinces and in America. Alternating with it, he played Gadshill in *Henry IV*.

At this time he was enormously high-spirited and full of zest, enjoying life with a light-hearted fervour. He encountered pain for the first time when his father died. The du Mauriers were an unusually close and devoted family, bound together by ties far stronger than any they achieved with the outside world and suffering acutely when separated. Immediately after his father's death he went to America with Tree on his first and rather unsuccessful tour. He found it expensive and he did not care for the people.

He began now to exhibit a susceptibility to women which showed itself in two abortive engagements – the first to a young French actress named Marguerite Sylva, the second to Ethel Barrymore. Later, when he left Tree, he joined the management of Mrs Patrick Campbell at the Royalty Theatre and remained with her, playing in London and on tour, for two years. Daphne du Maurier wrote:

> There was no peace with her, no quiet moment; it was either heaven or hell, ecstasy or despair. When you were with her you wanted to be away, out of sight, alone; and when she was gone it was torture until you heard that voice again, rather full, rather sullen, the voice of Athalie or Phèdre. You adored her and hated her in turn. You sat at her feet and worshipped, or rushed from her presence slamming the door and calling damnation upon her name. She was disturbing and possessive and impossible, but it was better to be frowned upon by her than ignored.

Also she taught one to act.

> Much of his charm, his delicacy, his ease of manner, and his assurance he owed to her. She worked tirelessly, taking infinite pains with him. . . . There were scenes, of course, blistering rows and fierce reconciliations, days of sulky silences and days of riotous successes. And in this weird mixture of excitement, anger, and frequent disillusion, Gerald developed his mind, his intuition, and his little grain of genius.

'I have taught a clown to play Pelleas,' said Mrs Campbell.

Then suddenly in the autumn of 1901 the company broke up: Mrs Campbell went off to New York and du Maurier at the age of twenty-nine, rather changed and showing for the first time the streak of bitterness which his later associates were to recognise as a part of his nature, returned home.

For a while he rested, playing in a comedy called *The Country Mouse* but taking life easily. Then in the following summer he was engaged to play the juvenile lead in Barrie's new piece *The Admirable Crichton*. Playing opposite him was a young actress named Muriel Beaumont.

Muriel Beaumont – known for the rest of her life as Mo – had much of the temperament of her mother-in-law, a temperament necessary to the du Maurier men. From the time that she married Gerald, she sank her own life in his, caring for no one but him and his children. In return, in spite of a susceptibility to women which caused his children to speak of the 'stable' and bet on the runners, he loved no one but her. Only when one of the runners, misunderstanding the situation and believing that she might seriously endanger the position of his wife, acted on this assumption, did his succession of love affairs impinge in any way on Mo's life.

The year following du Maurier's marriage saw the first performances of *Peter Pan*, which was written for his nephews (his sister's children), the Llewelyn Daviesies. Du Maurier doubled the parts of Mr Darling and Captain Hook. Daphne du Maurier wrote of his first performance:

When Hook first paced his quarter-deck in the year of 1904, children were carried screaming from the stalls, and even big boys of twelve were known to reach for their mother's hand in the friendly shelter of the boxes. How he was hated, with his flourish, his poses, his diabolical smile! That ashen face, those blood-red lips, the long, dank, greasy curls; the sardonic laugh, the maniacal scream, the appalling courtesy of his gestures. . . . Gerald *was* Hook. . . . He was a tragic and rather ghastly creation who knew no peace, and whose soul was in torment; a dark shadow; a sinister dream; a bogey of fear who lives perpetually in the grey recesses of every small boy's mind. All boys had their Hooks, as Barrie knew; he was the phantom who came by night and stole his way into their murky dreams.

Thus he reverted for the last time to the melodramatic past, to the world in which he himself had grown up, to the imitation of Irving and Tree in which he had so long excelled. The following year he appeared in *Raffles*.

Raffles was a gentleman and a cricketer but a cracksman. This was the first play about a crook and it was the first example

of 'naturalistic' acting. To quote Daphne du Maurier once more:
'He brought something to it that was personal and unique – a
suggestion of extreme tension masked by a casual gaiety –
making of Raffles someone highly strung, nervous, and finely
drawn, yet fearless and full of a reckless and rather desperate
indifference, someone who by the force of high spirits had
developed a kink in his nature.' This might be a description of
du Maurier himself; it was the part he was to play for the rest
of his life both on and off the stage. How much of it was
natural, how much 'naturalistic', no one would ever know. His
critics, most of whom have arisen since his death (unlike Kean
and Irving who had to wait on posterity for complete recognition, Gerald du Maurier won great appreciation in his lifetime),
quite rightly insist that there is a difference between the two.
Whether in the theatre this difference is always clear is
another matter. Ultimately the art of acting – as also the art of
writing plays – is to seem to be rather than to be, and styles
that to one generation seem natural may to the next seem
naturalistic. Actors often appear to be playing a part and,
when one enters a room and hears a voice on television reply-
ing to the questions of an interviewer, one can normally tell
when it belongs to a member of the acting profession. The timing
is invariably too good, the modesty – so desirable on television,
yet so difficult to achieve – too easily handled, the lines thrown
away in a manner impossible to the ordinary man. Spending all
his professional life in impersonation, the actor finally loses
his own identity and becomes naturalistic rather than natural –
a tendency which becomes more obvious as fashion and
mannerisms are no longer in the style of the day. Now that
actors of the past can be seen on film or television, great talent
reveals itself, more than in any other way, by the extent to
which the mastery of the performer transcends the inevitable
changes of fashion.

Gerald du Maurier has two great claims to fame. The first is
that he invented the 'naturalistic' manner, and in doing so
killed the melodramatic manner which had become an obstacle
to the presentation of the 'new' drama and even to acceptable
portrayal of the classics. He put the modern meaning into the
theatre word 'ham', and, although he has been followed by
actors who have been able to adapt his technique to the require-

ments of the classics – even high tragedy, a feat he never attempted – it remains true that he made a vital contribution to the development of acting.

His second claim to fame is that, within the limits he imposed upon himself, he was a master. Beloved by the public, he was nevertheless an actor's actor. Only another actor is fully aware how difficult is the style he made his own and, just as people say of Picasso that he can draw and paint in the traditional style when he wishes, so everyone in the theatre knew that du Maurier could play every part to perfection. He left behind him one convincing record. He was one of the first to appear in a 'talking' film when the technique had been sufficiently developed to leave behind something like a true impression. An extract from his film, *Lord Camber's Ladies*, made in 1932, produced by Alfred Hitchcock and directed by Benn Levy, was shown in 1969 in the television programme *Omnibus*. Watching this extract and asked to comment on it were Sir John Gielgud, Dame Edith Evans, Donald Sinden and Vanessa Redgrave.

Du Maurier played the part of a doctor and held a glass in his hand.

'Give me the nitric acid,' he said to Benita Hume, playing opposite him, and when she did so he dropped it into the liquid in the glass and asked her if she could see it cloud.

'No,' she replied after an interval.

'Neither can I.'

Miraculously, in the last three simple words, their impact undiminished, were all the wit, style and individual timing which had made du Maurier supreme in his day. Commenting, Dame Edith Evans said:

He was a very, very fine actor indeed. He could do every part Better than they did. But he chose to be the sort of originator of the rather throw-away style, which when it didn't have the guns behind it, which it had when he did it. . . . A lot of people copied him; all they did was throw away, but they didn't throw anything away, do you see. I'd great admiration for him.

His success in *Raffles* was the turning point in his career. He followed it with *Brewster's Millions*, *What Every Woman Knows*, *Arsène Lupin* and *Alias Jimmy Valentine*. Most of these were trifling plays, poorly written, but the public, who still preferred great acting to great plays, filled the theatre to see du Maurier. The pattern of the future was set.

In 1909 he produced, although he did not play in, his brother Guy du Maurier's play *An Englishman's Home* at Wyndham's Theatre, under Frank Curzon's management. *An Englishman's Home* was one of those extraordinary pieces of timing for which generation after generation of du Mauriers have shown such flair. It was the story of what happened to a middle-class Englishman and his family, untrained to bear arms, when England was suddenly and unexpectedly invaded by enemy troops. Mr Brown refuses to leave his home, is found with a gun he is unable to use competently, is captured and shot by the enemy after a foolish, useless but gallant display of patriotism. Three or four years later *An Englishman's Home* was as dead as if it had never been written, but at the time of its production it touched some response of fear and horror in the audiences and, received with a frenzy of enthusiasm, was regarded by those responsible for England's defence as the finest piece of propaganda ever written.

In 1910 du Maurier joined Frank Curzon in management at Wyndham's Theatre and with only one break remained at this theatre for most of his acting career. The break was occasioned by the war.

He was a natural leader of men and his skill as a producer has been testified to again and again by the leading actors and actresses of his day. He could play each part in every play – in *The Dancers* it was said he vaulted backwards and forwards over a bar at rehearsal while instructing two of the younger members of the cast – and his natural manner and faultless sense of timing became part of the technique of modern acting and could be seen not merely in his own performances but also in those of actors like Ronald Squire and actresses like Gladys Cooper, Tallulah Bankhead, Celia Johnson, and hosts of small part players who owed their style to hours of patient coaching at Wyndham's Theatre.

Nevertheless, the thing that most distinguishes him from every other actor-manager of his eminence is that during the whole of his career he was responsible for no production of any historical interest whatever. He introduced no play which has remained in the repertory of English theatre and he neither acted in nor produced any of the classics. He said of himself that he was the lowest of the low-brows and this was the simple truth. The age in which he lived was inexplicably philistine, the tastes of audiences returning to the level of the audiences of the early nineteenth century – 'the winter solstice' of the British drama. From Tree to Barrymore no one dared to risk Shakespeare in the West End of London, no reliable public existed for opera, which was put on only at the expense of philanthropists, musical comedy replaced light opera because even this proved too strong a diet for popular consumption, and the word 'highbrow' was adopted in denigration of anyone whose tastes were other than the most trivial. An analysis of the underlying causes of such a situation is a matter for social historians but in such circumstances it is not entirely surprising that the great gifts, the extraordinary stage presence of the leading actor of the day, should all have been wasted on productions of purely commercial drama.

The most notable production of his career was that of Barrie's *Dear Brutus*. The story of the artist who is given a second chance in life but wakes to find this a dream appealed to something in du Maurier's own nature and Daphne du Maurier wrote of his performance in this play:

Those who watched Gerald as Harry Dearth in 1917 saw, not a performance of an imaginary character, but the revelation of a living man, his hopes, his fears, his little ghosts and dreams, what he might have been, what he might yet become, a challenge and a confession in one. . . .

It was very moving and very terrible; he concealed nothing, and laid himself bare to the gaze of the world with a ruthless disregard of his own privacy, putting himself in pillory, to be looked upon by the curious as though in some sudden and desperate need of salvation.

But this was a rare occasion. For the most part du Maurier put his talents to the service of light entertainment.

Whether a sense of the triviality of his professional career contributed to the discontent and despair which finally overwhelmed him it is impossible to say, because this inability to enjoy life is so often the price paid for creative talent. It can be found in the melancholia of Dr Johnson and Evelyn Waugh, the aching nostalgia of George du Maurier and Ruskin and heard in Graham Greene's confessions of boredom. In Gerald du Maurier it caused a strain of bitterness and self-pity to develop in what had been in youth a purely joyous nature.

During the war years when Tree went to America, du Maurier naturally took his place as leader of the theatre. He became President of the Actors' Benevolent Fund and during the whole of the war he performed valuable services for charities as well as providing in his professional capacity entertainment for the wartime population and the soldiers on leave. His wartime productions included *The Ware Case* by George Bancroft, the son of Squire and Marie Bancroft and *A Kiss for Cinderella* by J. M. Barrie. Then in the summer of 1918, at the age of forty-five, he joined the army. His military service lasted only a few months but this could not have been foreseen at the time he joined and the unnecessary, almost Wildean masochism of the act did not diminish its gallantry. As an example to the profession of which he was the head the gesture was entirely wasted and he seems to have been a very bad soldier. His daughter wrote of this period in his career:

It was impossible to teach him; he would not concentrate, and, as he had done at Harrow thirty years before, he was inclined to shrug his shoulders at authority and make humorous remarks at serious moments. The instructors found it easier to ignore him than to waste precious time in expounding theories which obviously meant nothing to him, and which he did not grasp.

Yet one cannot help believing that if one of his instructors had been called in to Wyndham's Theatre to guide its leading actor in the impersonation of a young cadet he would have found a lively intelligence which responded quite easily to instruction.

Luckily the ordeal was soon over and du Maurier returned to Wyndham's Theatre, to *The Choice*, *The Prude's Fall* and *Bulldog Drummond*. In January 1922 he received a knighthood for his services to the Theatre and to the Actor's Benevolent Fund.

These were the days of the luncheon parties at Cannon Hall the beautiful house in Hampstead where, because he could never be alone, the du Mauriers entertained every weekend. People were asked to lunch because they could play tennis, or because they were old friends or because he had been in the mood to ask them when he met them in the street, but they all had one quality in common. In some way they were connected with the theatre. Du Maurier had no interest in social life as such, and neither aspired to nor could be cajoled by what remained of high society. People flocked in and out of Cannon Hall all day on Sundays but the only conversation that could ever be heard concerned in one way or another the theatre.

At the centre of these conversations, at the centre of this world, du Maurier reigned as Irving and Tree had reigned. He had all the intense magnetism of his great predecessors, all the natural charm; he was lightly malicious, restless, bitter and discontented. He was adored by the men and women who surrounded him, adored and feared.

Among these was the playwright Frederick Lonsdale. Younger than du Maurier and coming from a world which gave him none of the actor's natural advantages, he was always in thrall to the older man. As a youth he had made a name for himself as a writer of musical comedy, and du Maurier with a characteristic mixture of affection and malice, usually referred to him as 'the muck writer'. Nor when Lonsdale began his enormously successful career as a writer of drawing-room comedies did he appear to be much more impressed. The sensitive relationship between these two men was the immediate cause of a break in theatrical tradition.

In 1923 du Maurier had a great success with a play called *The Dancers* which he wrote himself in collaboration with Viola Tree. Two previously unknown young actresses, Tallulah Bankhead and Audrey Carton, appeared with enormous success and together with du Maurier drew audiences for over a year. But this was the last of the great Wyndham's successes and du Maurier for the first time in his life had a serious run of failures. He was badly in need of a play to restore his fortunes when Frederick Lonsdale arrived at Cannon Hall to read him his new play, *The Last of Mrs Cheyney*. The two men dined together with Mo and after a good dinner and a glass of port retired to du Maurier's library where Lonsdale, settling down by the fire, began to read his play. Presently he looked up in expectation of intercepting some reaction from du Maurier to find that his host had fallen asleep.

He was not the first, nor, in all probability, the last man to fall asleep during the reading of a play, well known to have a disconcertingly soporific effect. The trouble in this case was that Lonsdale, who valued du Maurier's opinion above all else, did not believe he had fallen asleep. He believed him to be staging an insult. Furiously he rushed from the room and down the stairs, with Mo after him explaining that du Maurier was tired and ill, begging him not to break up a friendship of so many years, and, getting into his car, drove off to London. Unable to forgive du Maurier he gave *The Last of Mrs Cheyney* to Gladys Cooper who, in conjunction with Gilbert Miller, put it into rehearsal at the St James's Theatre.

There are two equally good male parts in this play and Ronald Squire was engaged for one of them. The part of Lord Arthur Dilling had not yet been cast when to everyone's astonishment a message was received from du Maurier saying he would like to play it. So *The Last of Mrs Cheyney* opened on 22 September 1925 with a quite exceptional array of stars and ran for 514 performances. The significance of the incident was that the play made a fortune, a fortune that but for du Maurier's slumbers might have revived the management at Wyndham's. His sleep closed his long career there, and with it the whole of an era. The great days of the actor-manager were drawing to a close and nothing could for long have prolonged them. *The Last of Mrs Cheyney* might have done so for a few more years.

Frank Curzon died soon after, however, and even more serious, so did T. B. Vaughan, his business manager. Without a theatre, without a partner or a business manager, du Maurier had to fend for himself. At various theatres during the next years he produced *Interference* by Roland Pertwee and Harold Dearden which was a financial success, a moderately successful revival of *Dear Brutus* and another of *Peter Pan*. He went back to Wyndham's for a short time, where he turned Edgar Wallace into a playwright by the education he gave him while producing *The Ringer*. With the money he made from this he bought the house at Fowey where his wife lived after his death. He produced a play called *Cynara* with Gladys Cooper in which Celia Johnson made a great success and he went on tour with George Bancroft's play *The Ware Case*, a tour during which he made little money for himself but over £100 in every town for the Actor's Benevolent Fund. As late as 1932 he acted in *Diplomacy*, first put on by the Bancrofts in the 1880s. But everything now was an effort and success obstinate and grudging. Daphne du Maurier writes:

For the first time, Gerald began to look a little older, a little weary, a little worn. He complained of not sleeping, of feeling eternally tired, of having 'Mummie's pain' under his heart. . . . He spent much of his time pottering in the drawing-room and looking through old letters of Guy's, old sketches of papa's. It was as though he wanted to soak himself in the past and shut away the present and the future.

Fewer people came to the Sunday lunches. He began to appreciate quiet days. . . . Here he was, at the head of his profession, nearly sixty and sick to death of acting; frittering away the days in doing nothing, in lunching with a pal, in having a yarn, in hanging about; wondering at the back of his mind why he was alive at all, and if there was any riddle in the universe after the long day was over. And, in spite of everything, he had to go on acting because he could not afford to retire.

He could not afford to retire because, like so many people after him, now that he was into the lean years he began to receive tax demands for money made in the fat years. This was a new and unexpected hazard in a profession already too hazardous. He felt trapped and to earn money he began to play small parts in talking films.

Nowadays, when one sees an old, beloved and respected actor or actress playing bit parts in films, one rejoices that, for a few weeks' work each year he or she is making enough money to live on. No longer the one-night stands, the long train journeys, the desperate attempts to play men or women the age of one's grandchildren. For a few weeks, up much too early, standing about all day, speaking a few lines – then peace and security. But when du Maurier played the doctor in *I Was A Spy* and a valet in *Catherine the Great* audiences held their breath in pain to see the mighty so fallen. 'He loathed every poisonous moment, it was something that had to be endured. . . . He did it because he could not at the moment bring himself to consider any other means of making money; it was one stop-gap after another, one more straw floating on the surface of the water.'

Then the day came when Sybil Beaumont, his sister-in-law and secretary, presented him with a new tax demand. 'I can't be bothered with income tax, Billy dear', he replied. 'They're probably quite decent fellows. Write and tell them I haven't any money.' He began to drink too much brandy and his gaiety was almost gone. In 1933 he died. He had struggled too hard to carry on a tradition which in the conditions of the day was already out of date. He left very valuable property in Cannon Hall and the house at Fowey and, when all was settled, it was found that Mo was sufficiently well provided for.

Epilogue

In 1969 the Arts Council Grant to the National Theatre was £340,000 and to the Royal Shakespeare Theatre Company £200,154. The Royal Shakespeare Theatre Company reported a deficit of £161,126 and stated that they faced the biggest financial crisis since they started in 1928. No moral can be drawn from this except that expressed in Tree's elliptical definition: 'When is a repertory not a repertory? When it is a success.' (He meant that the only way the expenses of a repertory company can be met is by abandoning the policy every time a play is sufficiently successful to be kept on for a run.) Nevertheless, if it is financially no easier to run a repertory of serious plays today, this makes an interesting point from which to review the achievement of the actors who managed the theatres of London for fifty years or more.

Without either patron or state aid, they had to please the public if they were to keep their theatres open. They were scolded by the critics for a lack of adventure in their choice of plays and for a lack of taste in their productions. They refused to put on Ibsen and they caused Shaw to invent the word 'bardicide' and to accuse Irving and Tree of turning to Shakespeare as to a forest out of which literary scaffolding 'could be hewn without remonstrance from the landlord'. Nevertheless, from Bancroft to Tree they kept Shakespeare on the boards of the theatres and gave production to such new English playwrights as came their way. The Bancrofts gave memorable productions of *The Merchant of Venice* and *The School for Scandal* and Irving of *Much Ado About Nothing*. Irving and Forbes-Robertson gave distinguished performances of Hamlet and Tree

put on an annual Shakespeare festival at Her Majesty's
Theatre. Alexander gave the first production to plays by Wilde,
James and Pinero, Tree to plays by Wilde, Bernard Shaw and
Pinero.

They kept the theatre alive in the provinces, touring themselves in the summer and keeping first class companies touring
all the year. (In addition to the leaders of the theatre, Sir John
Martin Harvey and Sir Charles Wyndham toured regularly in
the provinces and Sir Nigel Playfair had a glorious reign at the
Lyric Theatre, Hammersmith.) Irving, Tree and Forbes-Robertson travelled extensively in America.

Very few parallels with today can be drawn because the
conditions were so different, but certain principles for the
management of a commercial theatre emerged. In this book the
aspect of management has been dealt with only in relation to
dramatic productions because, while there was no universal
financial system and a high degree of financial chaos, the success
of a theatre depended then as now only secondarily on the
competence of the business management which was usually
carried on by a paid employee. Trying to explain how it was
possible for a theatre to be successful under Tree's inconsequent
management, Shaw said: 'Theatre business is not like other
business. . . . A London West End theatre is always either making such an enormous profit that the utmost waste caused by
unbusinesslike management is not worth considering, or else
losing so much that the strictest economy cannot arrest the
process by a halfpenny in the pound.'

The first rule for success in the Theatre is to choose a play
the public will pay to see. The second, equally simple and early
discovered by Bancroft, is not to run it too long. A. E. W.
Mason says:

Alexander was quick to understand when a play was sagging
because of one of those temporary depressions which once or
twice or even more often in a year afflict the theatres of London,
or whether it was dying. If it was dying he was no less quick to
whip it off before its vitality was quite exhausted. It was characteristic of the Grand Panjandrum that the gunpowder ran out of the
heels of his boots. That is nothing to the money which runs out of
a theatre when a play is kept on after its popularity has gone.

The third rule of the nineteenth-century theatre was that

in a star theatre the star must appear. Alexander could no more keep a theatre running profitably than Irving could when he was prevented by illness from acting himself.

Perhaps the last of these three rules accounts for the fact that, while there are few parallels with the present day, there is one curious parallel between the lives of so many of these actor-managers. With the single exception of Irving, they all became bored with the theatre. The Bancrofts retired in their middle forties and lived as long again in retirement without apparently wishing to return except occasionally to the stage; Forbes-Robertson retired at sixty and lived a private life for twenty years without regrets; Alexander continued to manage his theatre until his last illness but turned increasingly to politics; and Max Beerbohm noticed in Tree 'an impatience of his work'. Gerald du Maurier suffered a more embracing boredom – he was bored with life. It seems most likely that they were all exhausted by the everlasting need to entertain a capricious public.

The actor-managers were vital to the development of the English drama. By the strength of their personal characteristics they brought the middle and upper classes back into the theatre and changed the conditions and status of their profession. They introduced new standards of production and of acting, and without state aid kept a repertory of classical plays in production, while also putting on the stage the work of English playwrights of talent. They set up schools for dramatic art and established a benevolent fund for the members of their profession. They added colour to the social scene and invested the theatre with magic.

Bibliography

Archer, William, *Henry Irving, Actor and Manager*, Field and Tuer, 1883.

Arthur, Sir George, *From Phelps to Gielgud*, Chapman and Hall, 1936.

Bancroft, George Pleydell, *Stage and Bar*, Faber and Faber, 1939.

Bancroft, Squire and Marie, *The Bancrofts On and Off the Stage, By Themselves*, Richard Bentley, 1888.

Bancroft, Squire and Marie, *The Bancrofts*, John Murray, 1925.

Beerbohm, Max, *Around Theatres*, Rupert Hart-Davies, 1953.

Beerbohm, Max, *More Theatres*, Rupert Hart-Davis, 1969.

Craig, Edward Gordon, *Henry Irving*, Dent, 1930.

Craig, Edward Gordon, *Ellen Terry and her Secret Self*, Samson Low, Marston, 1931.

Dark, Sydney and Grey, Rowland, *W. S. Gilbert. His Life and Letters*, Methuen, 1924.

Dent, Alan, *Mrs Patrick Campbell*, Museum Press, 1961.

Du Maurier, Daphne, *Gerald, A Portrait*, Gollancz, 1934.

Forbes-Robertson, Sir Johnston, *A Player Under Three Reigns*, T. Fisher Unwin, 1925.

Great Acting, ed. Hal Burton. BBC. 1967

Gielgud, Sir John, *Early Stages*, revised edition, Falcon Press, 1953.

Hatton, Joseph, *Henry Irving's Impressions of America*, Samson Low, Marston, Searle and Rivington, 1884.

Henry Beerbohm Tree. Some Memories of Him and His Art, ed. Max Beerbohm, Hutchinson, 1920.

Irving, Laurence, *Henry Irving: The Actor and His World*, Faber and Faber, 1951.

Irving, Laurence, *The Successors*, Rupert Hart-Davis, 1967.

James, Henry, *The Complete Plays of Henry James*, ed. Leon Edel, Rupert Hart-Davis, 1949.

James, Henry, *The Scenic Art*, ed. Allan Wade, Rupert Hart-Davis, 1949.

MacCarthy, Sir Desmond, *Drama*, Putnam, 1940.

MacCarthey, Sir Desmond, *Theatre*, MacGibbon and Kee, 1954

Manvell, Roger, *Ellen Terry*, Heinemann, 1968.

Mason, A. E. W., *Sir George Alexander and the St James's Theatre*, Macmillan, 1935.

Menpes, Sir Mortimer, *Henry Irving*, Adam and Charles Black, 1906.

Ormond, Leonée, *George Du Maurier*, Routledge and Kegan Paul, 1969.

Pearson, Hesketh, *Beerbohm Tree: His Life and Laughter*, Methuen, 1956.

Pearson, Hesketh, *The Last Actor-Managers*, Methuen, 1950.

Pearson, Hesketh, *The Life of Oscar Wilde*, Methuen, 1946.

Pemberton, T. Edgar, *The Life and Writings of T. W. Robertson*, R. Bentley, 1893.

Playfair, Giles, *Kean*, Reinhardt and Evans, 1950.

Robertson, Graham, *Time Was*, Hamish Hamilton, 1931.

Rowell, George, *The Victorian Theatre*, Geoffrey Cumberledge, Oxford University Press, 1956.

Scott, Clement, *From The Bells to King Arthur*, John Macquean, 1897.

Shaw, Bernard, *Our Theatres in the Nineties*, Constable, 1932.

Steen, Marguerite, *A Pride of Terrys*, Longman, 1962.

Terry, Ellen, *Ellen Terry's Memoirs*, preface and notes by Edith Craig and Christopher St John, Gollancz, 1933.

Terry and Shaw, *Ellen Terry and Bernard Shaw. A Correspondence*, ed. Christopher St John, Constable, 1931.

The Oxford Companion to the Theatre, ed. Phyllis Hartnoll, 3rd edition, Oxford University Press, 1967.

Wilde, Oscar, *The Letters of Oscar Wilde*, ed. Rupert Hart-Davis, 1962.

Index

Figures in italics refer to illustrations

DATE DUE